Window Style

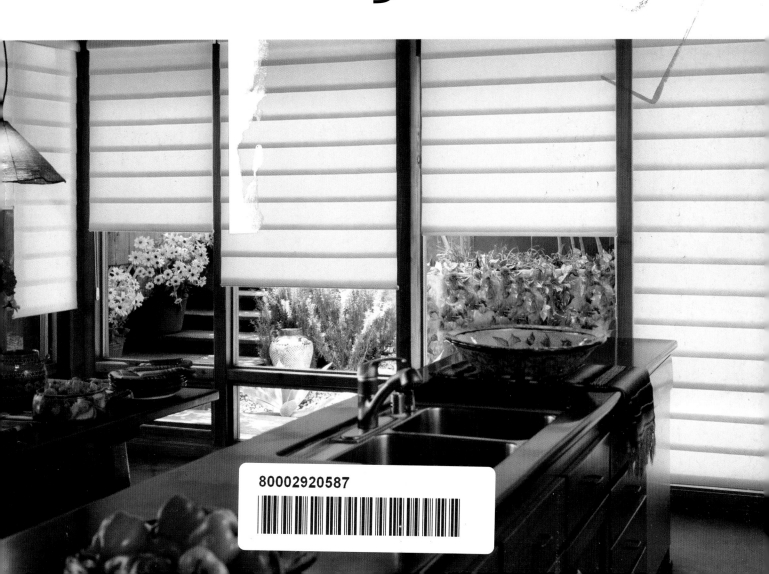

Window Style

500 inspirational
ideas for curtains,
blinds and fabrics

GINA MOORE

APPLE

First published in the UK in 2008 by
Apple Press
7 Greenland Street
London
NW1 0ND
United Kingdom
www.apple-press.com

A Marshall Edition
Conceived, edited and designed by
Marshall Editions
The Old Brewery
6 Blundell Street
London N7 9BH
www.quarto.com

Originated in by Hong Kong by Modern Age
Printed and bound in Singapore by Star Standard Industrial (Pte) Ltd

ISBN: 978-1-84543-246-1

10 9 8 7 6 5 4 3 2 1

Publisher: Richard Green
Commissioning editor: Claudia Martin
Art director: Ivo Marloh
Senior designer: Sarah Robson
Project editor: Deborah Hercun
Design and editorial: Seagull Design
Production: Nikki Ingram

Front cover photo: Andreas von Einsiedel/Designer: Michael Reeves
Back cover photos: *left* Andreas von Einsiedel/Designer: Catherine Warren; *right* Anthony Harrison/
Redcover.com; *front flap* Silhouette® window shadings from Hunter Douglas; tiebacks from Price & Co.;
back flap Christopher Drake/Redcover.com Architect/Designer: Philip Wagner

Introduction 7

Introduction

Can you imagine a house without windows? It's impossible; it would be a barn or a warehouse or a factory. But a house – your home – has to have windows. On a practical level, we need windows to let in light and fresh air, but they give us more than that; they are literally our 'windows on the world' – our connection to the outside world once we are at home. Through a window we have an idea of what time of day it is, what season it is, and what the weather is like; they connect us to our neighbours and neighbourhood, and to the wider world outside our door.

Windows form a focal point in most rooms. Walk into an empty room, and your eye is instantly drawn to the windows. The way we dress a window has a huge impact on a room's style, mood and atmosphere. The style and shape of the curtains or blinds and the colour, texture and design of the fabric you use, as well as decisions about accessories and hardware, are all vital aspects of décor. How you choose to decorate a window also reflects a large part of yourself – the way you live and your tastes. The design possibilities are endless, and restricted, in many cases, only by your imagination.

Decisions about what window treatment to choose are also based on practical considerations: the function of the room in which they are situated, be it the kitchen, family room or formal dining room; the architectural style or shape of the window; the style and colour of other furnishings within the room; the choice of materials available; and, of course, your budget.

Unlined Roman blinds filter the sun's harshest rays in this bright and sunny living room, while flowers embroidered onto the heavily interlined silk curtains at sill height are an unusual touch that helps to balance the overall look.

In this book we will look at the issues involved in styling a window and show that by carefully considering them, you can choose a style that will suit your window, your home and you. The following chapters demonstrate the myriad styles available today by dividing them into eight distinct looks: contemporary, classic, eclectic, romantic, rustic, retro, global, and, finally, children's rooms. In each of these chapters there are detailed suggestions for adapting your preferred style to fit different shapes and styles of windows – so that, whatever the architectural style of your home, you will discover how to achieve your chosen look.

History

Until the late 16th century, the use of textiles in interior decoration was mostly confined to wallhangings and bed-hangings. Tapestries and richly embroidered fabrics were not used on windows at all, but were elaborately arranged around huge, four-poster beds. This may have been primarily a practicality to keep out the cold, but it was also a vehicle to display the wealth and position of the occupants. For example, Henry VIII and Anne Boleyn had a bed that measured 3 x 3 m (11 x 11 feet)!

The sight of windows hung with paired curtains became common in European homes only from the 17th century onwards. Style was dictated by the flamboyance of the courts, aided by steady technical advances in the art of textile production and the economic impact of increasing world trade, beginning with the circumnavigation of the globe and widespread colonisation. The style of the 18th century was influenced by the excesses of King Louis XIV's court at Versailles in France, alongside the innovations developed by the highly skilled silk-weaving industry that had

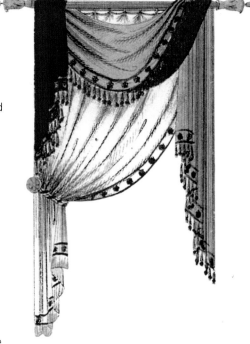

Above: A design for an asymmetrical curtain with swag dating from the French Empire period at the start of the 19th century. Interior style was heavily influenced by Napoleon's Egyptian campaign.

Below left: Heavily curtained four-poster beds were a vehicle for displaying the wealth and status of their occupants.

Below: An elaborate window treatment design from the Victorian period when several layers of curtaining was the fashion.

been established in Lyon. By the start of the 19th century, Napoleon Bonaparte's military campaigns in Egypt inspired the touches of Middle Eastern flair that were assimilated into the French Empire style of the period.

During the 19th century, a growing middle class, wishing to display their affluence, favoured a flamboyant, heavily trimmed approach. This style often involved several layers of curtains at the window, including ruched sheer curtains, lighter curtains that were drawn, and heavy dress curtains with elaborate trimmings and heavily swagged valances and cornices. This taste for overabundance reached almost ridiculous levels by the end of the Victorian era, when fabric covered all available surfaces, from doorways to mantelpieces.

Toward the end of the 19th century, an Englishman named William Morris started the Arts and Crafts design movement. The aesthetics of this movement were a reaction against the indulgent style and advocated a return to basics, inspired by a romanticised medievalism with simpler naturalistic textile designs and much less complicated window arrangements. Although not everyone adhered religiously to his strict principles, he had a huge influence on interior design.

The 20th century saw a steady progression of styles, often closely aligned with periods in art and clothing fashion, starting with the romantic, stylised naturalism of Art Nouveau at the turn of the century. The Art Deco period of the 1920s and 1930s was influenced by trends in modern art and architecture. This was widely disseminated through the new medium of the cinema, both in the architecture of the movie theatres being built in every town and city, and in the glimpses of Hollywood style that the movies themselves portrayed. The austerity of wartime utilitarianism in the 1940s gave way to the optimistic modernism of the 1950s and the pop art exuberance of the 1960s and

1970s. During the 1980s, an economic boom encouraged a look of conspicuous consumption, to which the minimalism of the 1990s was a direct response.

Now, at the start of the 21st century, we are in an enviable position, able to cherry-pick from a variety of styles that have been influenced by historical periods, art and technology, as well as ethnic styles from around the world.

Above: A classic printed textile design by William Morris dating from the second half of the 19th century – his designs were influenced by his interest in the medieval period.

Left: A room designed in the Art Deco style of the 1920s and 1930s, which was influenced by movements in modern art as well as by the cinema.

Light

The main function of any window is to allow natural light into a room. However, we have the option of modifying that function with curtains and blinds and, in order to do that effectively, consideration must be given to the kind of light available and the way in which you hope to use or alter it. To start with, this depends on geographical location. In hot seasons, we may want to filter the light in order to control the temperature indoors and offer relief from the relentless sun outside. Opaque sheer curtains diffuse bright light, while slatted blinds or shutters control the angle of the light and create moody shadows.

In colder, greyer seasons, we often welcome in as much of the little available light as possible, but we have to balance that with considerations about heat loss and energy efficiency. Heavy curtains that can be drawn at night to retain heat and create a cosy atmosphere inside need to be able to be pulled back during the day to allow in as much light as possible. And you may need to think carefully about the light that will be lost if valances or cornices overhang the window too far.

The direction that a window faces also has a bearing on light. A south-facing room will be filled with warmer, even fierce, direct sunlight, while a north-facing room will be cooler, with more diffused light by comparison. East-facing rooms will see more light first thing in the morning, and, correspondingly, west-facing rooms will receive more light at the end of the day.

The function of the room itself also has a bearing on the way in which we treat light. For instance, a kitchen will benefit from plenty of bright light, and fabric blinds that roll up and out of the way may

Above: The light from a north-facing window is indirect and cool.

Right: A south-facing window floods a room with bright and direct sunlight.

be a good choice. In a study, the ability to filter or redirect light away from computer screens may be a consideration, and, in that instance, a slatted Venetian blind could be the answer. Bedrooms need to be cosy and dark at night, so full-length curtains with a valance or cornice could work well.

Obviously, it also depends on personal preference – some people like to wake up in a light-filled room; others have difficulty sleeping unless all light is excluded from the room with heavy, lined curtains, or

'blackouts'. And it is also about mood. There are times when we welcome natural light in, and other times when we seek to diffuse and modulate it to create a more intimate or calming atmosphere.

To put it simply, the quality and quantity of light from a window needs to be considered carefully when you are thinking about window décor. And, in reality, it is often a combination of blinds, sheer curtains and heavy curtains that allows us the flexibility to control light at different times of the day and during different seasons of the year.

Function

After assessing light, thought must be given to the other functions that a window,

and the choice of window treatment, perform. Some windows look out onto a stunning view, be that urban or rural, and, as such, only need to form a frame for that view. Blinds that roll all of the way up, or other minimalist treatments, might be all that is needed. But other windows look out onto less inviting scenes – a busy street or a brick wall – and, in those cases, the window treatment needs to form a screen between the interior and the exterior. Sheer or lace panels, together with heavier curtains with elaborate trimmings or rich fabrics, will not only screen the view, they will also help divert the eye away from the depressing scene outside and back into the room.

When it comes to privacy and security, do not forget that while we want to be able to see out of a window, we do not want curious eyes from outside prying into our homes. Sheer fabrics and lace made up into panels, café curtains or full-length curtains will allow light into a room while maintaining privacy. At night, when the lights are on inside, sheer panels alone are not enough to protect privacy, so, in some cases – in a bedroom or bathroom, for example – it is more convenient to have a roller blind that can be pulled up and down easily and on demand, instead of opting for more cumbersome curtains.

Security issues must also take account of how a window is secured, especially when we are not at home. Security gates and shutters are necessary in some cases, and care must be taken not to obstruct them with complicated window treatments. On the other hand, gates in particular are not very attractive, so we

Right: This blind is made from a semi-transparent, high-tech 'solar' fabric that actively deflects light and heat, protecting furnishings from fading and helping to maintain cooler indoor temperatures.

may wish to obscure them behind more aesthetically pleasing fabrics.

During the winter, an important function of window treatments is to insulate a room against the cold outside. The draught from gaps in windows and doors, as well as the loss of heat through the windowpanes, will be minimised with a well-made pair of interlined curtains. And there are thermal linings that improve performance in this area considerably. Conversely, in warmer circumstances, thought must be given to eliminating heat from a room. Blinds, such as Venetians or Romans, can help by blocking the sun's rays altogether, but there are also high-performance 'solar' fabrics that are used for roller blinds. In spite of their transparency, such blinds can effectively deflect heat and glare so that it is possible to see out of the

Noise is another matter to take into account. If you live on a noisy street, then dense, full-length, interlined curtains will help reduce the noise level that penetrates the room when they are drawn – vital for peaceful bedrooms. Alternatively, in contemporary, minimalist interiors with so many hard surfaces, such as uncarpeted floors, noise from inside the room can occasionally be the problem. Curtains have the ability to absorb sound, and the heavier the fabric and the more substantial the interlining, the more effectively the curtains will reduce the noise level from within a room.

Finally, we need to remember that a window needs to open – how often may depend on the temperature outside – to allow fresh air to circulate. How the window opens should be considered when choosing window coverings. Some modern windows even swing open into a room instead of out (the reason being that they are easier and safer to clean). An overhanging hard cornice, or other treatments that obstruct the top of the window, would be out of the question in that situation. French windows and doors often open into a room, and in some cases a portiere curtain rod that opens with the door is the answer.

Fabric: colour, texture and pattern

The starting point for a decorating scheme can sometimes be a particular colour or fabric that you have been dying to use. At other times you may be at a loss about what and how to choose from the thousands of different fabrics available today. Ultimately, it is a matter of taste

window at the same time as controlling the temperature indoors.

While still on the subject of regulating temperature, radiators are another factor that needs to be considered when deciding on window treatments. Although done for perfectly rational reasons from the point of view of a heating engineer, radiators are often placed beneath a windowsill, and this can create a quandary. Do you have short curtains that end on or just below the windowsill, thereby encouraging warm air from the radiator to rise straight up the back of the curtains

and out through the window? What if you prefer the look of full-length curtains that will block the radiators completely? There are solutions other than moving the radiator to another wall. One solution is to opt for blinds rather than – or even in addition to – curtains, since they are placed closer to the window and therefore minimise the gap through which the heat can escape. In the case of short curtains, building a shelf above the radiator, or a radiator box that entirely encases it, will direct the heat out into the room instead of up and behind the curtains.

or personal preference, and usually your budget has a bearing on your choice of fabric. However, there are some broad rules we can apply to the process.

Looking at colour, we can roughly divide them into either warm or cool shades. Reds, ochre yellows, terracottas, and olive greens are examples of warm colours. They will create a warm, inviting atmosphere and are good in rooms where there is a lot of activity, such as kitchens and living rooms.

Blues, especially paler blues, blue-greens, and lilacs, are cool colours. They will create a cool, restful, quiet atmosphere, and are a great choice for rooms that we like to use as sanctuaries – bedrooms and bathrooms, for example.

Of course, there are always exceptions to the rules, and there is no set law when it comes to decorating. Sometimes a strong accent or contrast will liven up a colour scheme. Imagine a strong red

used as a narrow contrast border on cool and pale blue floral curtains in a peaceful bedroom. Or a pale eau-de-nil green trim used to lift a rich burgundy curtain in a warm dining room.

Then there are the neutrals – white and cream through to oatmeal and taupe and finally black, that can be used together in a neutral scheme for a great effect, or in both warm and cool colour schemes. These colours break up or neutralise other stronger colours, to create a resting place for the eye. Some decorators insist on restricting window treatments to neutral colours alone and then giving cushions and throws, paintings and flowers the task of introducing colours into a room, so that these can be changed and added to as mood and fashion dictate.

Next it is important to look at texture in fabric – and that also includes what is referred to as weight (whether a fabric is lightweight or heavy). As a general

rule, heavier fabrics are better suited to full-length, more structured formal curtains with pinch-pleated or goblet-pleated headings that mould the fabric into deep folds. Fabrics such as velvet, damask, textured cottons and linens all fall into this category. Lightweight cottons, such as chintz and voiles, are more suited to simple gathered and sheer headings, making more casual, breezy curtains. It is important when designing window treatments to consider how a fabric will hang – whether it has a soft handle and drape that would hang well as a curtain, or whether it is crisp and unyielding, and therefore possibly best suited to blinds.

Adding lining and interlining to a fabric will alter its weight and may alter its drape.

Below left: A cool colour scheme that uses pale blues and greens is accented here with a pale pink.

Below: A warm and inviting colour scheme of reds and deep pinks against a neutral background.

Left: A neutral colour scheme of creams and dark chocolate is highlighted with a touch of red.

Below: The weight, fibre content and weave of a fabric affect its texture and the way light plays on its surface. A soft chenille ①, a cut-velvet spot in chartreuse and purple ②, a washed silk taffeta ③, an embossed silk damask ④, a linen and viscose basket weave ⑤, an unbleached linen with a random woven stripe ⑥.

Lining adds body to a flimsy fabric, while interlining – a layer of soft wadding that lies between the face fabric and the lining – adds weight, thickness and body, to create luxuriously heavy curtains.

Texture affects the way that light plays on a fabric – the sheen of chintz, the texture of linen, the nap of velvet and the shimmer of some synthetic fibres are brought to life by the varying intensity of both natural and artificial light. A plain silk, for example, can be transformed into something much more interesting when the folds and pleats of a curtain or blinds are caught in the light.

Patterns on textiles can be woven, printed, or embroidered. Woven designs include traditional and formal brocades and damask, as well as more 'utilitarian' stripes, plaids and checks. Printed designs are usually applied to flat, nontextured fabrics, which can be silk, cotton and linen, and there is an almost endless variety of designs, from subtle two-tone toile de Jouy prints to

①

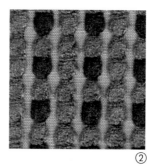

②

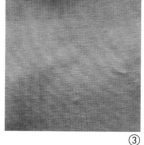

③

④

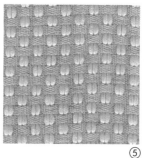

⑤

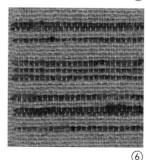

⑥

the modern bold prints by the Finnish designers Marimekko. Embroidered fabrics range from traditional, handmade crewel work through to intricately embroidered silks and some of the newer machine-embroidered cottons and linens. Embroidered fabrics are almost always floral in design.

When considering patterned fabric for curtains, it is important to remember that the flat sample in the pattern book will look different when it is hung in the folds and pleats of a curtain. Stripes will look less rigid, bold patterns will be softened, and some small patterns may be lost. And it is necessary to keep in mind the impact of a

Right: Pattern can be woven, printed or embroidered onto a fabric. A silky damask weave ①, a woven linen stripe ②, a floral tapestry weave ③, a traditional print on linen ground ④, a two-tone print on lightweight linen ⑤, a delicate print on a white cotton ground ⑥, a richly embroidered silk taffeta ⑦, one-colour machine embroidery on an unbleached linen ground ⑧, an embroidered synthetic dupioni ⑨.

pattern once it is repeated across a large expanse of a full-length curtain.

Always look at a fabric in as large a piece as is possible before you choose, to fold it and gather it in your hands to see how it drapes and how that affects the pattern. In the case of blinds and panels where the fabric will be displayed flat, you have to think slightly differently – where will the pattern sit in relation to the top and the bottom of the blind? Try and centre the pattern as much as possible.

Budget

The budget you have in mind for your window treatments will undoubtedly have a huge bearing on your final decisions. For most of us, curtains and blinds represent a significant expenditure, and adequate

forethought is essential in order to prevent costly mistakes. Well-made curtains should last a long time, so it is important to guard against going for the most fashionable option. Fashion is, by definition, changeable and, as such, it is not a particularly sound foundation on which to build a decorating scheme. It would be smarter in the long run to opt for a timeless and classic window treatment, and for fashion to be introduced with the other accessories in your room, such as cushions, throws and ornaments.

Remember that blinds use a lot less fabric than curtains, so you can usually afford to push the boat out slightly farther when choosing fabrics and 'trade up' to something more expensive and of a higher quality. The smart use of borders on curtains can also stretch a tight budget

a lot farther. The current trend for using deep horizontal borders, for example, could be interpreted by a careful designer as a golden opportunity to eke out an expensive textile with a low-cost one to create an overall effect of luxury and grandeur.

Another tip is to use interlining to add body to cheaper fabrics – a simple cotton calico will be transformed into a thick, lush, heavyweight curtain once it has been padded out with a layer of soft interlining between the lining and the face fabric.

However, it is important that, when it comes to window treatments, you should spend as much as you can afford. In the long run, a well-designed, well-made pair of curtains is as much about allowing you to control your environment as it is about making a personal style statement.

Window types

When it comes to styling window treatments, the first thing to consider is the window itself – its shape, size, position and aspect. The treatment you choose should suit the proportions and design of the window. Stand back and study your uncurtained window, weighing up its qualities as well as any difficulties it may present in regard to a proposed treatment. Every window has a unique character often integral to the architecture of the building. There are, however, some broad categories of window type into which most windows can be grouped:

Sash: This is a traditional window, most often with two frames – or sashes – of glass that slide up and down on a cord and weight mechanism that is concealed in the window frame. In some sash windows both frames, or sashes, can move up and down in the frame, but in others the top frame is stationary and only the bottom frame can slide. When both sashes can slide, the frames can be moved to the middle, leaving the window open at the top and the bottom to maximise air circulation, with cool air entering the room at the bottom, and warm air rising to escape at the top. Sash windows are usually taller than they are wide. They are elegant and suitable for most styles of curtains or blinds.

Casement: A casement window has one or two frames of glass that are vertically hinged to open inwards or outwards. In the UK and Europe casement windows often use projection friction and locking. If the frame opens inwards, the treatment you choose must not obstruct the opening of the window. Whether

Sash window

Casement window

Picture window

traditional or modern, this type of window suits most styles of window treatments. Sometimes, where space is limited on either side and the casement opens inwards, two separate blinds directly attached to the frame is the most suitable solution.

Picture: Wider than they are tall, picture windows are usually very large and occasionally also incorporate sash, casement or sliding window frames. In most cases these windows are suitable for all styles of curtains, although tracks and rods should be extended beyond the frame if possible, so that there is room for the curtains to draw back. Valances or cornices can be useful to create a feeling of height. Picture windows can sometimes be too wide for a single blind, but if the window itself is divided up into smaller frames, individual blinds for each section can work well.

Small window

Small: Some windows are so small, you must be careful not to overwhelm them with complicated arrangements. Valances and cornices with curtains on both sides can make a window look larger than it is, but if it is a very small window, sometimes a minimal treatment, such as a roller blind, or obscuring the glass with translucent adhesive film, or etched or stained glass, is a better solution.

Tall
window

Tall: Tall windows are envied and admired. High enough to be able to carry off grand statements such as swags and tails or elaborate valances, they suit both ornate and minimalist styles. If they are really high, the practicalities of drawing back the curtains must be considered. A curtain track with a cord or draw rods on the leading rings of a curtain rod are solutions. Alternatively, consider using a roller blind behind more formal curtains for on-demand privacy and light control.

Arched: Beautiful to look at, arched windows can present a considerable challenge for any decorator. For a formal treatment, handmade pinch- or goblet-pleated Italian-strung curtains can be made to fit an arched window, although a considerable amount of light and view will be lost. A simpler treatment is to leave the arched top of the window clear and only cover the lower rectangular section of the window with curtains or a blind. If light control is required, in a bedroom, for example, the arched top can be filled in with stationary fabric ruched into the centre. Alternatively, wooden shutters can be constructed by an expert carpenter to fit the arch, with louvred slats for light control.

Arched window

Doorway

Doors and doorways: Some doors have glass panels, and where these panels are etched or stained glass, curtains are not usually required. But in some cases where the glass is clear, either blinds attached to the door itself or sheer curtain panels ruched onto a bar at the top and the bottom of the pane will maintain privacy. Curtains are often used on doors and doorways to reduce cold draughts and conserve energy. Portiere rods that open with the door are very useful in these circumstances.

French windows: French windows are glazed double doors that usually open inwards. Traditionally, in France, these are accompanied by external shutters, which control light and security, so that only the lightest, unlined – often sheer – curtains are required indoors. In the absence of shutters, heavier curtains are more common, and these must draw back far enough off the window that they do not impede opening the doors. Where space on both sides is restricted, blinds attached to each door may be the best solution.

Sliding doors: A modern equivalent to French windows, sliding doors are usually sliding panels of full-height glass and can be very wide, in some cases extending to the full width of a room. Sometimes the space between the top of the door and the ceiling is also restricted, so careful thought must be given to the means of support for a curtain arrangement. Corded curtain tracks that are attached to the ceiling are discreet and, provided they are attached securely, will support curtains across a wide expanse.

French windows

Sliding doors

Bay window

Bow window

Bay and bow: Bay and bow windows are usually large and imposing and are designed to maximise the amount of light entering a room. Finding the means of curtain support can be challenging, since tracks and rods have to be bent to fit the corners and curves of the windows. Corded tracks are more practical, but are often not very attractive, so valances and cornices can be used to hide them. Rods that have to be custom-built to fit the contours of the window are expensive, and the cheaper store-bought alternative of rods with flexible elbows are only really suitable for lightweight curtains. Care should be taken to extend tracks or rods beyond the window as much as possible, in order to allow curtains to draw back far enough to allow as much light into a room as desired. In contemporary interiors blinds are a simpler solution.

Skylights: Skylights are usually set into sloped or flat ceilings and are an excellent way of increasing light in a room. Panels of fabric can be attached to them in a variety of ways to control light, but the

Skylights

most practical and effective way of dealing with skylights is to have custom-built blinds secured to the frames of the window itself.

Dormer: Dormer windows are built into the structure of a sloped roof and usually have very little room around them for curtains. Blinds attached to each windowpane, or drapery arms that are hinged to open inwards are two possible solutions.

Corner: Corner windows are often found in homes that have been converted. Where smaller rooms have been created out of larger ones partition walls occasionally extend very close to a window, presenting problems for the decorator. Single curtains drawn to one side, or simple blinds, are the solution. Wrap-around corner windows, where the window extends around the corner of a room, are increasingly popular in modern architecture. These present many of the same problems as bay windows in choosing the method of support.

Dormer window

Window in a corner

Wrap-around corner window

Contemporary

For many of us, modern life is fast-paced and hectic. At its best, contemporary style can provide an antidote to that perplexity by creating a sense of calm and order. An essential element in any contemporary decorating scheme is minimalism – the look is pared down to the bare essentials, with clean, uncluttered lines and sleek surfaces that foster a feeling of space and airiness.

Windows are vital in creating this sense of spaciousness, but it is important to retain the spirit of minimalism when choosing window treatments for a contemporary setting. Blinds or shutters are the obvious unobtrusive option, but curtains are sometimes more appropriate, especially when a hard-edged scheme needs softening, or the insulating, sound-absorbing properties of fabric are necessary. Essential in creating a contemporary look is choosing fabrics, headings and accessories that are as sleek as the other elements in the scheme. Choose fabrics where the texture plays a more important part than the pattern. Opt for simple headings such as eyelet, tabbed or a neat cartridge-pleated heading that use less fabric, while holding it in undulating folds instead of deep pleats. In order to streamline the look, stick to sleek metal rods or discreet tracks built into the ceiling, or attach a hard, straight cornice that hides the support mechanism. Keep embellishments to a minimum and choose metal, glass or wood accessories to add a stylish finish.

With poles fitted close to the ceiling to emphasise the height of this elegant city living room, filmy white sheer curtains filter the light that floods through a double set of French windows.

Sash windows

The key ingredient to a contemporary style is a calm, uncluttered look, and this is easily achievable with the simple yet elegant traditional sash window. Three large sash windows set side by side in an alcove are given a contemporary makeover with Venetian blinds that screen the view and diffuse the light. Notice how the three blinds are hung very close together across the front of the alcove so that architectural details are eliminated and the windows appear to be one large window.

① ② ③

Venetian blind slats come in various widths and finishes. Here, cool, contemporary metallic finishes reflect light back into the room and are available in rich, modern colours: silver ①, sapphire ②, gold ③.

With their elegant proportions, sash windows can carry most styles. The trick is to choose fabrics that suit your style and colour scheme. Here, silks in rich, contrasting colours have been used for long, heavily interlined curtains. The contemporary twist is created by dividing the curtains halfway down with a deep horizontal border, emphasising the height of the window.

While a contemporary style favours simple, flat headings, sometimes a fabric needs to be shown off in the deep folds that pleated headings provide. Double pinch pleat ①, inverted pleat ②, fan pleat ③.

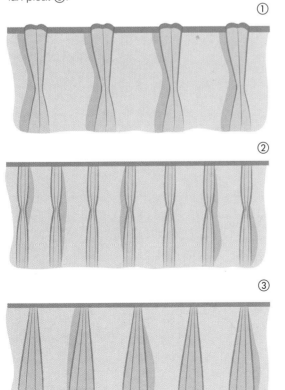

Picture windows

Picture windows are wider than they are tall, and you must allow for space on both side for the curtains to draw back. Another option is the clean, simple look of the Japanese shoji screen with sliding panels. Panels of fabric are weighted with a bottom bar and run individually along parallel tracks, which have been built into a wall or ceiling. This system enables them to file out across a wide picture window, or stack neatly behind each other. Here, sheer panels with wooden slats, reflecting a Japanese influence, run behind more opaque panels in a bold, printed fabric. Remember that space to stack the width of each panel is required on both sides of the window.

Sliding shoji screens are lightweight wooden frames covered with translucent paper. They are used in traditional Japanese architecture to conceal a window or partition a room.

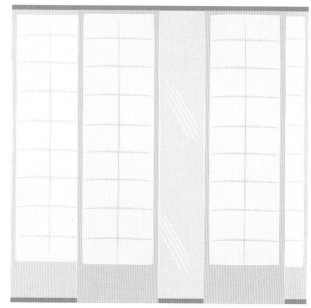

A neutral colour scheme is an essential element in a contemporary style. However, in the absence of colour, greater emphasis is placed on texture. Here, a tranquil bedroom has been created using no colour at all, but a deeply quilted throw and crisp sheets provide a contrast against the soft textures of the filmy sheer curtains and softly gathered linen at the window.

①

②

③

Neutral colour schemes place great emphasis on texture. A chenille with small motif ①, a sturdy cotton herringbone ②, a sheer with delicate outline embroidery ③.

Bay windows

The understated and uncluttered contemporary style is perfectly suited for the large and imposing bay window. Crisp, pleated Roman blinds are an excellent way to modernise this traditional window, creating a sense of space by allowing a lot of light into a room, while also leaving the attractive window frames exposed. Here, privacy is maintained with sheer, flat panels on the lower half of the windows. Although blinds are essentially minimal in structure, it is interesting to notice how a neutral, cool or warm colour scheme radically alters the mood.

Choose from the following alternative colourways. Dark neutrals ①, pale green/ blues ②, warm pinks/ oranges/reds ③.

Bay windows and bow windows allow a lot more light into a room than a flat window is able to, and this light-filled dining area is a perfect example. Plain white voile curtains soften the light that shimmers on the various reflective surfaces in the room. This bay window has five separate windows, and the voile curtains hang from individual rods that are attached to the top of each one. This avoids the complication of having a continuous pole made to fit the bay window, but it does restrict the curtains from being drawn all the way back to the sides of the bay.

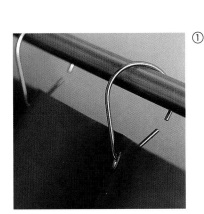 ①

 ②

Add interest to simple voile curtains by choosing unusual curtain rings. Droplet-shaped rings slide through small eyelets inserted in the top of the curtains ①, rings with small but powerful clips are a very simple option for holding lightweight curtains ②.

Casement windows

For a single alternative fabric, choose a texture that drapes beautifully. A subtle striped silk ①, a bright plain linen ②, a cut velvet stripe on linen ground ③, a textured chenille weave ④, a contemporary Jacquard silk ⑤.

①

②

③

Access must be considered when choosing your treatment for casement windows. Here, an understated elegance has been created with these full-length curtains, made from a patchwork of large pieces of coloured silk. Although long, these curtains are not overly wide, allowing the dramatic effect of the fabric to carry the look. As a rule for a contemporary look, curtain headings should be less full than would be usual for more traditional window treatments – think of single cartridge pleats, double pinch pleats, or even flat headings with eyelets or clip-on rings.

④

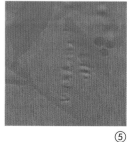

⑤

Contrasting with the historic architectural detailing in this room, with its high ceiling, cornicing and arched windows, a serene and modern interior has been created using neutral and natural materials with clean, simple lines. The cream muslin curtains framing the deep recessed casement windows are simple and understated, with flat, unpleated headings hung from rings on plain metal rods.

Pin-hooks help create minimal, unpleated headings. Spread the fullness evenly across the width of your window by using two curtain hooks for each ring on your pole, or glider on your track, allowing the fabric between the hooks to balloon gently outwards. A heading with pin-hooks – the front view ①, the same heading, from the back ②.

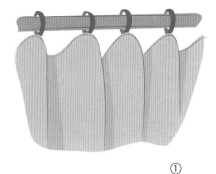

Stylish metal rods give a simple, modern look. Many rods are available now with metal, wood and glass detailing. Stainless-steel rods with chunky wooden rings, and wooden ball finial ①, and wooden lipstick finial ②.

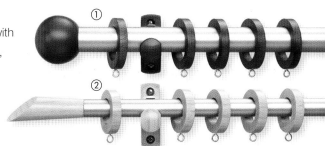

Two-storey windows

Two-storey windows will dramatically flood the room with light. Here, sliding panels in a large, graphic floral print hang alongside double-storey windows, accentuating the height in contrast to the low furniture. Choosing banner-like panels instead of curtains means that the print is in full view and not obscured by folds and pleats. By strictly adhering to a limited colour scheme and contrasting the print with bold, textured stripes and blocks of solid colour, none of the modernity and clean lines of the striking architecture have been compromised.

①

②

③

Bold, graphic prints can liven up a contemporary scheme – especially if they are used flat in blinds or panels so that the pattern can be seen in full. A two-tone print on linen ①, a contemporary floral print ②, an abstract leaf print ③.

A generous swathe of golden silk falls dramatically, unifying the double level of windows in this two-storey interior. The curtains have been given extra length so that the silk pools on the floor to balance the height and draw the eye downwards. Silk is an especially good choice for this window treatment. Because silk is so lightweight, it billows as it reaches the floor, while its intrinsic lustre catches the light. Adding detail to hems always looks best on full-length curtains, but attention must be paid to match the chosen window treatment to an appropriate fabric.

For alternative hems, horizontal pleats will add weight, volume and a crisp finish ①, deep contrasting borders add depth and balance ②.

Arched windows

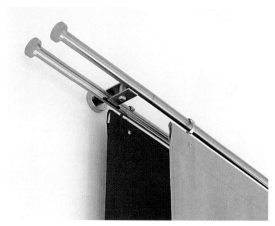

Metal battens with hooks are inserted into the slotted heading of a fabric panel and suspended from a wonderfully engineered double-rod system. Another batten goes into a slot in the hem to add weight and tension.

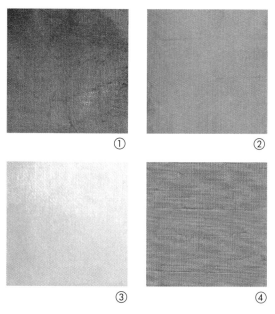

High arched windows are intrinsically beautiful and, especially in a contemporary setting, should be left alone as much as possible. Here, four contrasting banners of lightweight linen slide back and forth on an ingenious double-rod system to create a striking, versatile but minimal treatment for a pair of elegant arched windows. And, because the linen is slightly translucent, the detail of the windows is never lost.

For sliding panels, only lightweight unlined fabric should be used. A taupe silk taffeta ①, an eau-de-nil silk dupioni ②, an ivory silk velvet ③, a sheer sea-green linen ④.

Vertical blinds are a perfect contemporary solution for arched windows, especially since they can be custom-made to neatly fit within the contours of the arch. This is not only a practical solution; the blinds also beautifully define and accentuate the shape, while providing options for privacy and light control. On this mezzanine floor next to a huge arched window, the semi-translucent vanes can be flattened for privacy and maximum control of the sun's rays or opened to give a virtually unimpeded view of the outside world.

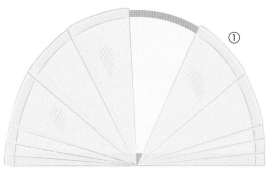

①

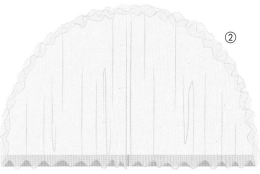

②

Variations for a large arched window could include a segmented fan-shaped blind ①, sheer curtains with a ruffled heading ②.

Corner windows

Windows that extend around a corner can pose a challenge due to limited space at that corner for accommodating window treatments. Here, the corner window is close to a doorway, making it impractical to use curtains. For the rare occasions that you would actually want to block out this tranquil harbour view, pull-down roller blinds in a vibrant floral print are concealed within a discreet recess above the window.

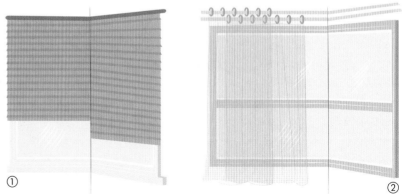

① ②

Alternative approaches could include Venetian blinds ①, a double track with two sets of curtain-ring-headed sheer curtains ②.

With corner windows, the visual harmony of the treatment should be considered. In a bedroom you need to consider privacy and light control, as well as providing a cosy setting. Here, sheer cellular blinds can be adjusted to let in light while maintaining privacy, while full-length curtains soften the atmosphere and unify the varying window levels. The clever part is that the two curtains are two single curtains instead of a pair; they run in one direction, but on separate tracks, so the hardware doesn't have to negotiate around the corner.

① ② ③

Sleek contemporary curtain options could include a cut velvet on linen ground ①, a lustrous cotton/viscose weave ②, a contemporary Jacquard weave ③.

Problem windows

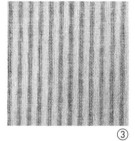

Sheer curtain
alternatives could include
a sheer silk with an
embroidered floral design
①, a floral lace ②, a
striped semi-sheer ③.

Where glass reaches from floor to ceiling and from wall to wall, supporting your curtains can pose a problem. Curtain tracks can be mounted directly onto the ceiling – as long as they are securely attached, especially in the case of heavier curtains. Metal rods have a limited span between the brackets, so special 'C'-shaped passing rings are required to pass over brackets, allowing the curtain to be fully operational across the window. If there is no space at the sides of the window for a decorative finial, use recess brackets to attach the rod flat against the wall.

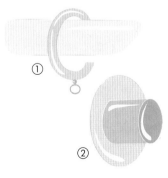

Wide-span poles
that reach from wall
to wall require special
fittings. Use passing 'C'
rings to traverse mid-
span brackets ①,
recess brackets ②.

The problem posed by a tall, narrow, floor-to-ceiling bay window has been solved here using neat and tidy vertical blinds contained within a sheer curtain. Providing the best of both worlds, this pairing combines the practicality of vertical blinds that can be rotated in the usual way to control light with the soft drapery of sheer curtains that can be drawn back in the same way as a regular curtain.

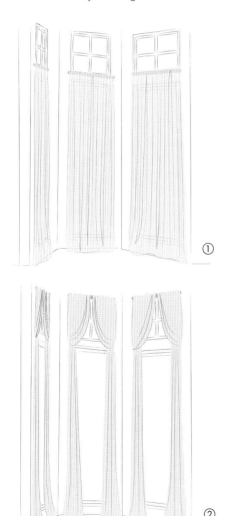

Blinds are not the only option here. You could use sheer curtains ①, heavier, Italian-strung curtains ②.

Classic

Window treatments in a classic style can range from tailored sophistication to grand opulence, but they are always generously proportioned and often richly embellished. While it is an obvious choice if you are decorating a period home, a classic style can also be adapted for a modern setting with great effect.

A classic style in soft furnishings can include deeply pleated or ruffled headings for fuller curtains, in some cases with elaborate top treatments such as swags and tails, shaped hard cornices, and loosely gathered valances. Blinds can also play a part, from ruffled Austrian blinds to simpler stagecoach blinds. Even roller blinds can be included in a classic interior, although with a shaped lower edge detail and usually also paired with curtains.

The key to achieving a classic style when dressing windows, as with all style choices, is to carefully consider your choice of fabrics, trimmings and hardware. If you are looking at plain fabrics, think about shimmering silks or deep-pile velvets, while traditional patterned fabrics include rich damasks, floral chintz, embroidered silks and crewelwork, as well as more restrained checks and stripes. And for a classic style with a contemporary twist, try some modern graphic prints.

Trimmings range from delicate, fan-edged braiding to heavy bullion fringe and tasselled tiebacks. More tailored decorative details include contrasting borders, both on hems and leading edges, as well as additional touches, ranging from coordinated covered buttons at the base of headings through to bows and rosettes. If the top of a curtain is not going to be hidden by a swag or pelmet, opt for traditional wood or wrought-iron curtain rods with ornate finials.

Classic with a twist – a graphic print in rich colours paired with a modern eyelet heading creates a bridge between the elaborate architectural detail in the room and more modern furnishings.

Picture windows

Full-scale picture windows can be overpowering if a busy or fussy pattern is used. Here, an understated elegance has been achieved by using lavish amounts of simple cream cotton in deep pleats, hung from wooden rods over light-controlling cellular blinds. The curtains have been cut to be overlong so that the fabric pools on the floor in sculptural folds. The key classic element here is the use of elaborately tasselled tiebacks holding the curtains in place.

Tasselled tiebacks are an important accessory to classic designs and are used to add colour, texture and a touch of grandeur. Brightly coloured twisted rope and tassels in red and green ①, a fine silk tassel in muted tones ②, a more elaborate knotted tassel ③.

A modern yet tailored classic look can be achieved by these imposing giant-grommet curtains threaded onto a simple wooden pole. The contrasted banding at the heading and hem accentuates the sharp tailoring. The curtains are paired with a functional Roman blind in a coordinating print.

For more traditional pleated headings, choose from cartridge pleats ①, goblet pleats ②, French pleats ③.

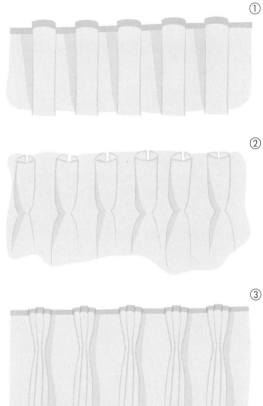

Use subtle classic fabrics for this look. A dark plain linen ①, an understated ribbed silk with trailing leaf woven pattern ②, a wide satin stripe ③.

①

②

③

Bay and bow windows

Hanging curtains in a deep bay window can be a challenging task, especially when there is very little space between the windows and ceiling to secure a rod. One way to solve this problem is to attach a rod straight across the opening to the bay window. This substantial wooden rod is sturdy enough to support sumptuous silk curtains with a deep cartridge-pleat heading, balanced by deep contrasted banding near the hem. If you feel that more functional light control close to the windows is necessary, use discreet roller blinds.

①

②

③

Patterned fabrics could work well here. Opt for a delicately coloured damask weave ①, a deep red fabric with flocked leaf design ②, a silk with embroidered feathers ③.

For a wide, shallow bay window with wall space above, there is room for an elegant top dressing, such as this rod with looped swags and tails, trimmed with tasselled fringing. Although richly decorative, this dressing also serves to hide the tops of the curtains, which can now hang from a functional corded curtain track for easier usage. And, with the rod attached higher than the top of the window, no light or view has been obscured. At the same time, the scalloped swags break the hard lines of the shallow window frame, creating an illusion of height.

Alternatives to the tailored swags shown here could include a multiple swag with pleated cascade tails ①, a swagged valance with flower rosette ②.

Sash windows

When two sash windows are side by side within a single framework, it makes sense to treat them as one. A subtle checked fabric in cool blues and cream has been used here to unify a pair of sash windows with a simple knotted swag over full-length curtains for a pretty, romantic look. Instant drop-down light control is provided by individual roller blinds at each window.

①

②

③

Change the mood dramatically by using a different colour palette. Graphic black-and-white stripes ①, warm terracotta and sage green floral ②, airy white and yellow sprig sheer curtains ③.

Sash windows are often taller than they are wide, and this means that they can carry classic styles that might overpower a less elegantly proportioned window. Here a highly curved, upholstered pelmet with flamboyant tasselled trim creates an imposing statement at a recessed window. The full, heavy curtains are held back with ornate brass holdbacks and embellished further with tasselled rope.

Decorative floral holdbacks, made out of either carved wood or moulded resin, are an alternative to rope tiebacks.

①   ②   ③

Classic styles like this can also carry a patterned fabric. A traditional damask ①, a repeat motif on linen ②, a dark printed silk embroidered with butterflies ③.

Corner windows

Windows that are too close to the corner of a room can be difficult to dress. Here the treatment has been kept narrow, with tailored plaid curtains hung from a wooden rod. The detail comes in the overhang, or attached valance, at the top of the curtains. This has been given definition with the use of a tasselled fringe, which draws the eye upwards and balances this slim look.

Attached valances can take many forms. A teardrop valance with tassels on an inverted pleat heading ①, a curtain-ring heading with a plain foldover ②.

①

②

Wooden rods are a key element of classic style and come in many different styles and finishes. These poles both have classic urn finials. An antique gold finish on a plain pole ①, an antique white finish on a reeded pole ②.

①

②

Chunky embossed metal finials add a touch of glamour.

Where space is limited between a window and the corner of a room, a single curtain pulled with a tieback toward the corner looks more balanced. Here a clever asymmetrical arrangement of swags with a single tail only falling on the opposite side to the main curtain not only gives balance; it also creates a harmonious unity with the rest of the windows in the room.

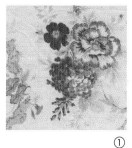

①   ②   ③

For a more feminine look opt for classic florals. A distressed print on linen ①, a taupe silk with embroidered trailing flowers ②, a traditional damask weave in a linen and cotton mix ③.

Arched windows

One way of working with an arched window or doorway is to ignore the arch and attach a rod below the curved section of the window. Here careful consideration has been used to choose a rod that matches the wooden frame of the doorway. Since the door opens inwards, the rod is longer to allow the curtains enough room to draw back out of the way. Adding a deep contrasting border that seems perfectly in proportion with the uncurtained arch creates a balanced composition.

Adding a contrasting border or other decorative details to hems adds interest, focus and proportion. An inset border with fringe down the leading edge and along the hem ①, an appliquéd contrast border along the hem ②, a deep contrast frill along the hem ③.

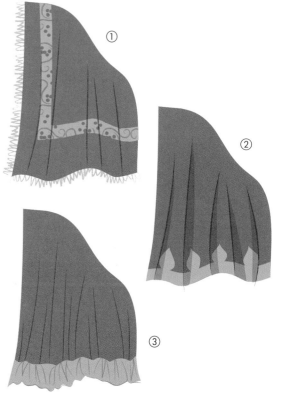

Rods made of wood come in many finishes including lime-washed oak ①, antique ivory finish ②, gold leaf ③.

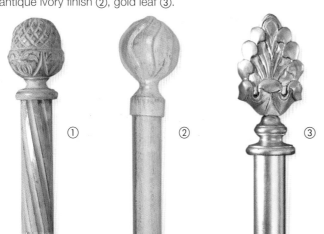

Where a classic, structured finish matches the style – and especially where privacy and light control is important – a stationary heading that has been skilfully built inside the arch works well. Here, gathered drapes with goblet pleats are held back with Italian stringing that lifts the curtains upwards and to the side, invisibly doing the job of hold-backs. However, this treatment will only work if the windows open outwards.

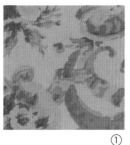
①

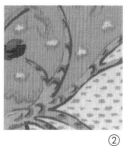
②

③

Add rich colour to your scheme. Choose a traditional print on tea-stained linen ①, a classic print on bleached linen ②, a rich red and gold brocade ③.

French windows

①

②

③

The height of French windows can be emphasised to great advantage when the right fabric is used. Here an imposing trio of French windows in a beautiful bow shape has been crowned with an ornate gold cornice, from which pairs of velvet drapes cascade to pool on the floor. Despite the splendour of the setting and the cornice, there is a casual artlessness in the way that the curtains lack trimming or tiebacks. The traditional wooden shutters behind them do the job of light control.

Holdbacks, like tiebacks, are used at the sides of a window to hold curtains back and come in various styles and finishes. Here an antique brass-finish holdback has a decorative floral design.

Alternatives to plain velvet could include a dark embroidered sheer ①, a cerise cut velvet on a natural linen ground ②, a shot taffeta ③.

Where both sides of the curtain are visible, as in this example on a French window leading into a garden room, double-faced curtains are necessary. And a tented tieback is a stylish way of displaying both fabrics together. A ring is sewn around two-thirds of the way down the leading edge of the curtain, which is then swept back into a tieback hook attached to the wall at the side.

Tented tiebacks can also work well with a holdback positioned quite low.

Instead of a tieback hook, use a holdback with a fabric loop on the leading edge instead of a ring. Sun holdback ①, flower holdback ②.

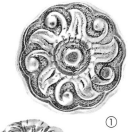

①

②

Casement windows

Cornices, whether wooden, upholstered or plaster, are an excellent way of enhancing or improving the proportions of a window. Here a moulded wooden or plaster cornice sits above understated Italian-strung curtains to balance a narrow casement window, as well as to conceal the curtain track and heading pleats.

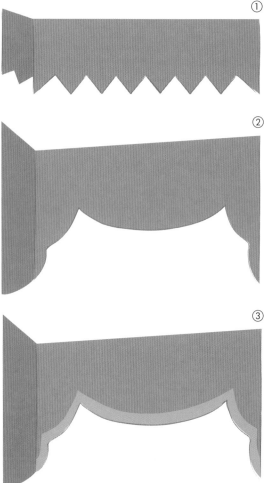

Shaped cornices provide interest and depth. Consider zigzagged ①, scallop-edged ②, scallop-edged with a contrast border ③.

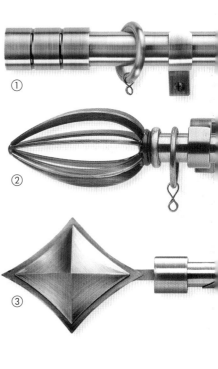

Brass rods can be brought up to date with modern finials. A ridged barrel ①, a cage ②, a diamond ③.

Headings can also be used to balance proportion. For these heavy, interlined dress curtains, the top of the curtain has been piped and folded over to form a structured ruffle that echoes the fabric pooled on the floor. Alternatively, instead of using piping, the ruffle could be edged with a twisted cord trim. A blind hangs within the recess of the window in order to control privacy and light.

①

②

③

For heavy structured curtains choose a soft chenille ①, a heavy linen and cotton Jacquard weave ②, an interlined silk dupioni ③.

Doorways

Curtains over doors can be used to block cold draughts, but this practical measure need not mean your doorway cannot have style! Rich black duchess satin with gold-braided trim has been used here to make these imposing door curtains with a valanced cornice. The striking black-and-white colour scheme replicates the photo gallery surrounding this doorway.

Valanced cornices are a classic ingredient for formal curtain treatments. A shaped cornice with ruffle ①, a box cornice with ruffle and with serpentined lower edge ②, a box cornice with onset swags, trimmed with fringe and rope ③.

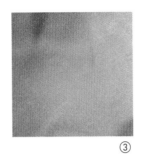

① ② ③

For a grand statement choose grand fabric. A cotton and wool woven medallion pattern ①, a shot silk damask ②, a gold satin ③.

To curtain off a doorway or opening between rooms, where curtains can be viewed and enjoyed from both sides, it makes sense to hang double-faced curtains. In this stately room two curtains have been used to create a great effect – drawing one curtain back with a tieback, revealing the contrasting lining of the other.

Peaked windows

Lighter colour schemes could feature an eau-de-nil embroidered silk ①, a pale green two-tone printed linen ②, a pale blue with white woven floral pattern ③.

①

②

③

Unusual windows, such as peaked windows, can be framed to great effect to highlight their shape. This floor-to-ceiling gable-end window has been given a classic medieval treatment by using two layers – a dark velvet curtain and a billowing sheer curtain. Both fall from gathers at the apex of the roof and are stapled to battens along the sloping walls and then pulled back with a pair of long tasselled tiebacks to form a shape that follows the line of the gable.

① ②

Part of the fun of tassels is that they can be 'over the top'. A flamboyant drop tassel in vivid colours with gold detailing ①, a rosette with a large tassel hung with smaller squab tufts ②.

A high conservatory is given a summery, tented look by using a fine striped cotton that appears light and sheer when hung unlined close to the glass. When lined, the same stripe appears much more substantial and is used for heavier curtains in the doorway and a deep zigzagged pelmet that echoes the shape of the peaked roof. Jute fringing and tasselled tiebacks complement the basket-weave furniture and frame the garden outside.

Trimming helps define the shape of a valance. A narrow contrasted border delineates the stepped inverted box pleats ①, droplet beads attached to each pennant elongate the shape ②.

①

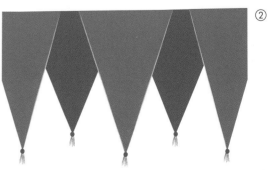

②

Eclectic

Words that define an eclectic style could include distinct, individual, imaginative, different and dramatic. It fuses together fabrics, colours, accessories and techniques in unexpected combinations. It is a style that defies convention; that is never dictated by tradition or fashion; that is always exciting, and sometimes even a little wild.

Eclectic style is a fusion of ideas from classic and contemporary designs, rustic and global style, but delivered with a twist using outrageous fabrics, vivid colour combinations, and flamboyant trimmings. While it can work well with the architectural details found in a period home, eclectic style can also help add vibrancy to the pared-down spaces of a modern building.

You can base your scheme on a particular fabric that you love – a wild print or an embroidered voile, perhaps. Or the inspiration can originate from a passion for colours and the way that they can play off each other. It may even begin with the art or accessories that you have collected and want to complement

or reflect in the other choices you make in decorating your home. Once you've chosen your fabric, think of displaying it in unusual ways – try tied-on headings, or threading a rope through eyelets inserted along the top edge of the curtain. Alternatively, you could hold the curtains back with a string of glass beads, a wreath of silk flowers or a plaited rope. Sewing pearlised buttons down the leading edge as a trimming will catch the light, while attaching tassels at the base of the heading pleats will create a sense of movement.

Whatever the inspiration, the key to a successful eclectic style is to think outside the box and juxtapose your choice with something surprising and exceptional.

The key to an eclectic style is to break all the rules. The softly ruffled, romantic curtains in this bedroom dramatically contrast with the vivid colour combination of hot pink, orange and electric blue.

Casement windows

To give a casement window a touch of the dramatic, use a single curtain and sweep it to one side with a sumptuous, tasselled tieback. You will lose some light from the window during the day with an arrangement like this, but, in some circumstances, that is not a crucial factor. The striped silk curtain has a goblet-pleat heading with brass buttons at the base of each pleat to match the narrow brass rod from which it hangs.

Tasselled rope tiebacks are available in a myriad of colours and styles. Beaded tassel tiebacks will catch the light and add an extravagant flair.

Casement windows can sometimes appear plain, so giving them an eclectic style treatment can be very effective. Here, panels of vivid green sheer fabric are alternately hung with a heavier, dark green cotton and slotted onto a rod above. Since slot-headed curtains don't draw back very easily, they have been pulled aside and held with fabric ties. Light filters through the sheer panels like sunlight filters through trees, complementing the animal prints on the furniture.

Consider alternative ways to tie back curtains. A standard arrangement with tiebacks on each side at sill height ①, a central arrangement with both curtains drawn to the centre with a single tieback ②, an asymmetrical arrangement where each curtain is held back with tiebacks at different heights ③.

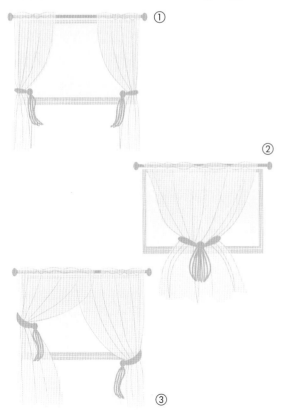

Fabrics that are lightweight and textured are ideal for this eclectic look. A sheer with woven medallion design ①, a crinkle sheer ②, a printed sheer ③.

Arched windows

Arched windows are a blessing for an advocate of eclectic style. Stylish and unusual, they make it easy to surprise the eye with an unexpected twist. Here, a subtle purple colour palette adds a touch of moody luxury to this bedroom. A dark sheer curtain printed with a large motif coupled with sensuous, purple satin, full-length curtains frame a trio of tall, arched windows with classic fan-shaped transoms.

①

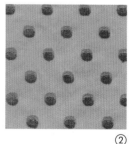
②

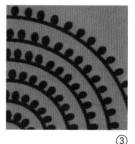
③

Fabrics with unusual colour combinations and textures suit eclectic style. A printed linen in taupe on white with splashes of bright pink ①, a velvet spot in pink on lime green ②, a shot blue taffeta with black flock dots ③.

An eclectic approach attempts to fuse disparate styles. The formal arrangement of furniture here belies an unusual colour combination of gold and purple, highlighted with black and orange. Two arched windows are elegantly delineated by vertical blinds in a deep purple vinyl to create a cohesive and structured composition of colour and shape.

①

Blinds that remain within the structure of the window frame are an excellent way of emphasising the shape of an arched window. A standard-shaped, pleated blind with a separate, stationary, fan-shaped blind for the arch ①, a standard-shaped, cellular blind with a separate operative blind for the arch ②, a Roman blind attached to a fabric-covered board for the arch ③.

②

③

French and sliding doors

Where space is limited beside a window for pulling back the curtains, keep the fullness of the curtains to a minimum. Here, unlined curtains with a curtain-ring heading have been made with narrow cartridge pleats to give them a manageable amount of fullness. The large checked pattern of the fabric reflects the other warm colours in the room, while a chunky, dark-stained wooden curtain rod echoes the strong horizontal lines formed by the black coving and picture rail.

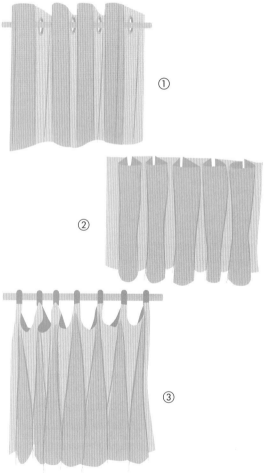

Stationary heading pleats hold the fullness in a curtain and create deep structural folds. Goblet pleats ①, box pleats ②, cartridge pleats ③.

In some cases screening the light rather than letting it in becomes the priority. This dining room in a modern extension has a glass ceiling that floods the area with light, and beautiful, black, sheer, embroidered panels have been hung on the sliding doors, filtering in a darkened view of the garden. They are tied onto a slender brass rod that is built into the narrow space between the top of the doors and the bottom of the transoms.

Metal rods are usually narrower in diameter than wood, which makes them very useful where space above a window is limited. They also look more graceful, especially when paired with delicate finials such as these. Flower finial ①, tulip finial ②, shepherd's crook finial ③.

For dark-coloured sheers, look for a plain ruby-red lightweight linen ①, a dark gold and brown horizontally striped sheer ②, a richly embroidered bronze on brown net ③.

Sash windows

Curtains with contrasting linings are a good way of achieving eclectic style because two colours can be used. A powerful statement in hot-pink fabric, these curtains on an elegant sash window are drawn back so that the contrasting orange lining is revealed and the fabric is held in place with braided tiebacks. The overall effect is to create a bedroom that, despite a nod to some elements of classic style, is a riot of colour, pattern and texture.

Various colourways could work in this room. Turquoise and green ①, red, white and blue ②, predominantly black, with silver and gold ③.

① ② ③

Fitting curtains where space is limited requires careful thought. In this narrow dining room, a single curtain made up of four separate drops of vibrant colours draws to the left so that it does not obstruct the cupboards on the right. Notice how the narrow metal rod in the confined space between the top of the sash window and the ceiling has been made extra wide, in order to allow the full curtain to draw off the window, allowing as much light as possible into the room.

① ②

③ ④

⑤ ⑥

Fabrics with graphic prints will work well in an informal dining room. Choose a large bold floral print ①, a flamboyant tulip print ②, a broken-wave stripe print ③, an embroidered floral print ④, a Chinese tea-cup print ⑤, a monochrome cutlery print ⑥.

Alternative approaches

Since eclectic style does not follow any rules, it is left to the imagination to find extraordinary solutions for your windows. This full-size flag serves as an unusual curtain to filter the light through a tall window in a relaxed and simple dining room.

Alternative and fun ideas for window treatments could include handpainted designs on the glass panes ①, simple curtains made out of plaid rugs with fringes ②, panels made of camouflage netting ③.

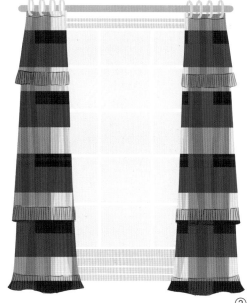

②

③

Here, an ingenious solution has been found for unwanted CDs by stringing them together and hanging them in strips in the window so that, as they twist and turn in the breeze, they reflect and refract light across the room, as well as acting like a screen.

Picture windows

In a room that has been designed around large picture windows, where there is no apparent division between the garden and the interior, heavy full-length curtains will define the limits of the space. These curtains in a bold, red-on-orange print can easily be drawn when a more enclosed atmosphere is required. To maintain the seamless division between indoors and outdoors, the curtain track has been built into a narrow recess in the ceiling so that it is completely out of sight.

Heading tapes that allow curtains to be pulled up into different kinds of pleats and gathers come in several forms. Narrow, one-inch gathering tape is set down a couple of inches to leave a gathered stand above ①, pencil-pleat heading tape gives an even, tailored finish ②, net-pleat tape is translucent, for use on sheer fabrics ③.

①

②

③

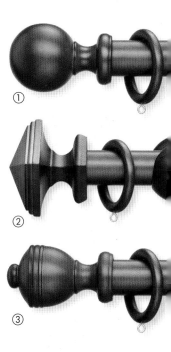

Choose strong shapes for finials on dark wooden rods. Ball-end finial ①, square finial ②, urn finial ③.

In some instances curtains are not intended to ever be drawn. For instance, at this large picture window the dark-stained, wooden Venetian blinds provide all the privacy and light control that is necessary for a bedroom. The choice of dark wood for the blinds and other accessories gives a sharp and sophisticated look to the warm red and gold colour scheme. However, in order to soften hard lines and create a cosier atmosphere, the boldly striped dress curtains, which have been tightly gathered directly on the rod with a slotted heading, are essential.

Fabric choice is vital for a rich but structured effect. Consider heavy weaves in bold colours. A lustrous herringbone linen mix in a deep pink ①, a multi-coloured stripe on cotton canvas ②, a textured velvet stripe ③.

Problem windows

Lightweight fabrics with bold and bright eclectic patterns are fun. Look for modern floral prints on a lightweight cotton ①, an embroidered silk ②, an embroidered lightweight linen ③.

①

②

③

Awkwardly shaped ceilings can mean there is limited space for window treatments, as in this bathroom with a pitched roof. If the casement window opens into the room, blinds are not the solution, either. Instead, a track has been attached to the wall directly above the window and hidden behind lightweight curtains in a gauzy, lime-green fabric, beautifully gathered with a puffed heading. When more light is required, the curtains are tied back with a bow rather than drawn back so that the track is not exposed.

Blinds are a good choice for awkward windows. A Roman blind in a sheer fabric looks crisp and neat ①, an Austrian blind in a sheer fabric looks soft and romantic ②, a stagecoach blind is simple and a good choice for blinds that are usually left pulled down ③.

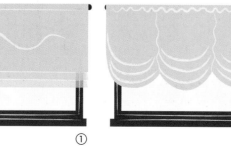
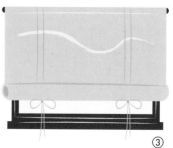

①   ②   ③

Space is limited in this bedroom, where the bed has been positioned between two tall, narrow windows, leaving very little room for curtains. The solution is a single curtain in each window, with a goblet-pleat heading and tasselled fringe down the leading edges. Notice how the round holdbacks from which the tasselled tiebacks have been suspended are set high up on each side, allowing the overly long curtains to be lifted as well as held back, thereby allowing more light into the room.

①   ②   ③

Fringes are a decorative way of softly defining the edge of a curtain or valance, as well as adding colour, texture and finish. A corded fringe ①, a two-tone, tasselled fringe ②, a delicate, beaded fringe ③.

Romantic

Romantic style is beautiful and feminine, and appeals directly to the senses with soft supple fabrics that invite the touch and gathers, frills and swags to charm the eye. It can be as simple as a rod-pocket heading or more formally structured with swags and tails, but the emphasis is always on the fabric and the addition of dainty embellishments.

Choosing the right fabric is crucial for capturing the romantic spirit in window dressing; in many cases, opting for delicate floral chintz, beautiful embroidered silk or gauzy lace is all that is needed to achieve this style. Fabric patterns range from romantic florals through to pretty stripes and checks. Romantic colours are muted and restful with splashes of soft pastel tones to highlight a predominantly pale and neutral colour palette. Appropriate fabrics are usually lightweight, but if a heavier fabric is required, hard lines can be softened with a pretty frill or fringe.

Trimmings are always a key element to romantic style – ranging from soft fringes to beads, feathers and even pompoms. One tip is to accent a romantic treatment with subtle sparkle and shine by using pearlised shell or glass-beaded fringes to catch the light. Romantic curtains need to be held back in a dramatic sweep, so choose delicate beaded and tasselled tiebacks or decorative wrought-iron holdbacks. Curtain rods can either be painted and distressed wood or traditional wrought iron although they should never be too heavy or dominant. There are several smaller accessories, such as pins and hooks, that will help to add a subtle touch of romance to the plainest window treatment.

Simple, unlined floor-length curtains in a soft and silky fabric soften the light to a romantic glow in a room with feminine and delicate furnishings.

Sash windows

Rod-pocket headings are simple and elegant and can be used for either flat panels ①, or gathered curtains with a ruffle ②.

In a bathroom it is important to go with practical options. Choose fabric that is preshrunk to withstand steam and splashes and, where possible, a curtain style that is easy to take down and wash. In this dreamy bathroom, where bulkier curtains close to the bathtub would be problematic, soft sheer curtains have been ruffled onto a rod and held with pretty tiebacks. For privacy, a flat, sheer panel slotted onto narrow brass rods at the top and bottom has been attached to the bottom sash of these sash windows.

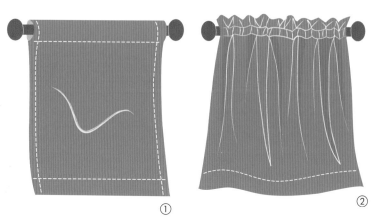

① ②

Curtains with a rod-pocket heading are usually stationary and are not intended to be drawn at all. For instant drop-down privacy and light control, hang a roller blind close to the window, especially one with an appealingly shaped bottom edge to suit the romantic feel. At this tall sash window, dress curtains in an embroidered silk have been slotted into tight gathers on a brass rod for a simple, romantic look.

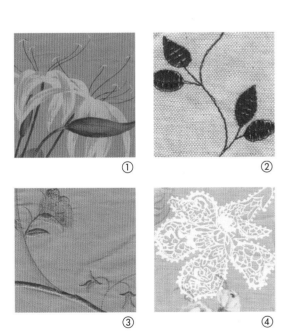

For romantic style choose fabrics that are prettily floral. A gold silk with handpainted lilies ①, a natural linen union with embroidered trailing leaves ②, a silk with gold embroidery ③, an embroidered cotton rep ④.

Bay windows

A romantic style can also be dark and sensuous, as this rich, floral damask fabric in dark shades of red and pink demonstrates. Made into deeply pleated, full-length curtains at a panelled bay window and coordinated with an array of striking pillows on the upholstered sofa, a smooth and tactile fabric such as damask makes a good choice.

① ② ③ ④

Opt for richly textured fabrics for a sensuous romanticism. A dark red chenille weave ①, a red and pink cotton damask ②, a rich satin damask ③, an embroidered cotton rep ④.

A light and airy room with a huge bay window such as this, however, requires a softer touch. A gauzy, pink, semi-sheer fabric has been chosen for simple curtains to draw around the bay window. Some curtain rods for bay windows come with flexible elbows that can be bent to fit around the corners, but they are really only suitable for lightweight curtains such as these.

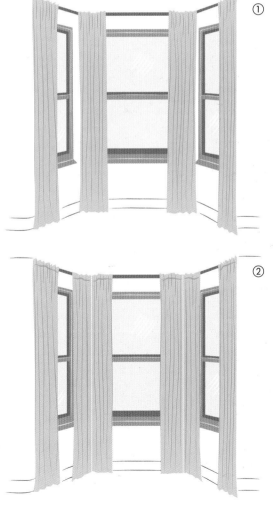

①

②

For a dainty, romantic touch, choose delicate beaded tiebacks to hold back lightweight curtains.

If your bay window is wide, with wall space between the windows, you can choose to hang four ①, or even six ② separate curtains in the window.

Picture windows

Borders are an excellent way to coordinate various fabrics in a room for a harmonious style. In a pretty bedroom, delicate borders have been added to the pale yellow cotton curtains in the windows. This matches the fabric of the embroidered sheer panels that have been slotted onto the posts of a four-poster bed.

For a fresh and natural romantic style, choose a lightweight cotton in a clean crisp check ①, a linen union with embroidered ferns ②, a pretty pastel printed stripe on cotton sateen ③.

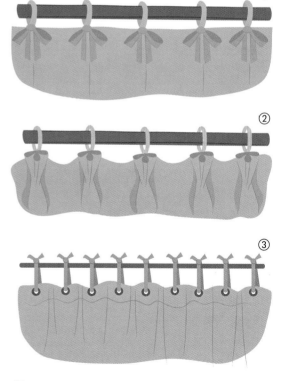

Sweet ways to add daintiness to a heading could involve using bow-tied loops ①, French pleats ②, a eyelet heading with ribbon ties ③.

At a picture window with a scenic outlook you need nothing more than a romantic scarf to frame the view. Choose an elegant wooden rod and wrap the prettiest lightweight, floral cotton that you can find in a simple double swag that drops to the windowsill on each side. Run a few tacking stitches through the folds of the fabric to hold the swags in place and stop them from slipping.

① 　　② 　　③ 　　④

Wooden rods come in many natural wood stains including natural ①, light oak ②, dark oak ③, mahogany ④.

Small windows

Gathered blinds are a delicate option that will suit small windows, as long as a lightweight fabric is used so that light can get through. This small, awkward window set into the eaves of an attic bedroom has been dressed with a deeply scooped cascade blind. Remember to make the blind longer than the window so that some fullness remains in the folds, even when the blind is let all of the way down to the windowsill. This kind of blind looks best if it is not raised too high.

① ② ③ ④

Traditional cotton floral prints make an ideal choice for romantically styled bedrooms. A classic print on a pink cotton/linen mix ①, a dainty floral print on a pink cotton/linen mix ②, a traditional glazed cotton chintz design ③, a pastel floral print on cotton sateen ④.

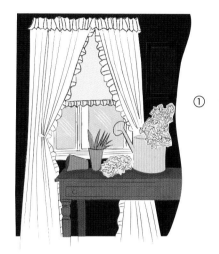

There are ways of making small windows seem larger than they are. In this room the curtains and blind have been attached slightly higher than the window, letting the curtains fall far below the windowsill, and the treatments are in a light, neutral shade that blends in with the surrounding wall. Both of these factors give the illusion of a larger window. The sweetly gathered cotton curtains have a ruffled rod-pocket heading with a short attached valance, and frills down the leading edges and across the hems, helping to give the window even more charm.

Choosing fabric colours that contrast with the surroundings will draw attention to the window, but may emphasise its small size. Pale neutral curtains with a dark wall ①, aqua printed curtains with lilac walls ②, deep magenta curtains with sage walls ③.

Casement windows

Casement windows have a simple look that suits romantic treatments perfectly. In this bedroom, curtains made from a lightweight cotton with narrow stripes and a ruffled rod-pocket heading are held back with tasselled tiebacks suspended from decorative metal hooks. A wide frill softens the line along each leading edge.

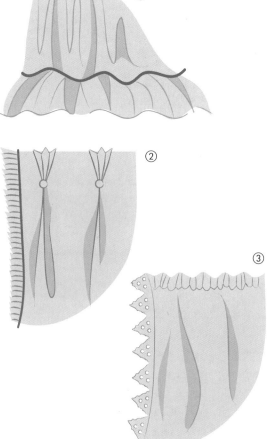

Attaching a frill to the leading edge of a curtain or the base of a valance adds an attractive, softening element. Choose from a frill in the same fabric as the curtains ①, a knife-edge pleat in a contrasting fabric ②, a readymade lace frill ③.

Decorative brass pins or tacks can be used to hold back the corner of a sheer or lace curtain in place of tiebacks.

Romance doesn't always have to mean a traditional treatment. Here on a pair of tall casement windows romance has been given a modern twist. Panels in a bold, gold-and-cerise-striped sheer fabric have wide horizontal borders across the top in a plain, opaque fabric, creating an indistinct impression of a valance, while also drawing the eye upwards to add a feeling of height.

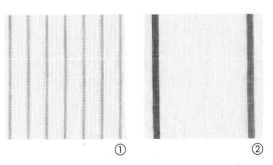

①   ②

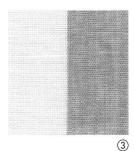

③

For a natural romantic option choose loosely woven lightweight linen. An aqua pinstripe on bleached ground ①, an alternate rose and mulberry stripe on bleached ground ②, a wide aqua and white stripe ③.

French windows

① ② ③

When French windows open inwards, ensure that there is plenty of room for curtains to draw out of the way when the doors are opened. Here, rich, red curtains hang at a pair of French windows. The plain-coloured curtains are given a narrow border of red gingham along the leading edge. This softens the line between the exterior view and the interior and adds a charming detail that coordinates with other furnishings in the room.

For a rich and structured look choose heavier weight fabrics with romantic floral prints or weaves. An unusual print of trees in reds and pinks on white linen ①, a finely woven sateen damask with pink flowers on an unbleached linen ground ②, a traditional stylised floral in white on pink linen ③.

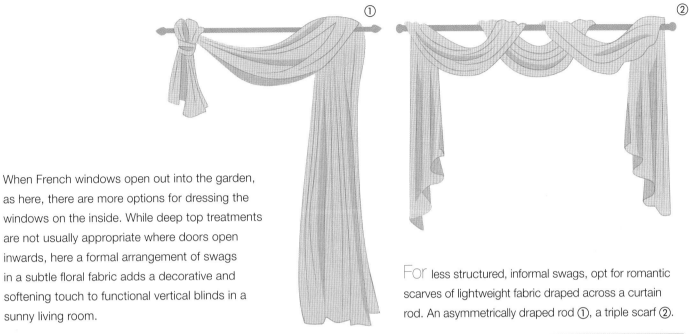

When French windows open out into the garden, as here, there are more options for dressing the windows on the inside. While deep top treatments are not usually appropriate where doors open inwards, here a formal arrangement of swags in a subtle floral fabric adds a decorative and softening touch to functional vertical blinds in a sunny living room.

For less structured, informal swags, opt for romantic scarves of lightweight fabric draped across a curtain rod. An asymmetrically draped rod ①, a triple scarf ②.

Problem windows

Lace will always be a favourite romantic fabric choice, particularly for bedrooms. A fern-pattern lace ①, a traditional rose-pattern lace ②, a wide-weave oatmeal floral lace ③.

①

②

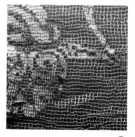

③

This window poses many problems. It is small and arched, with very little room above or alongside for rods or curtains, and the radiator and staircase below add even more obstacles. A soft, attractive solution has been found, using a pleated Roman blind in a sheer fabric on the rectangular part of the window, while filling the arch above with a stationary, gathered panel ruched into a central decorative knot.

A dormer window in the eaves of a steeply sloped roof needs to allow in as much light as possible. To give a low-ceilinged room a feeling of height in a romantic style, gauzy lace curtains have been slotted onto a rod built into the top of the dormer recess. Cute bow tiebacks hold the curtains in place at the point where the sloped ceiling meets the wall. Choosing a translucent lace allows light to flood in during the day, and a discreet blackout roller blind hung close to the actual window will provide light control at night.

Opting to keep the curtains closer to the frame of a dormer window means you have to hang the rod inside the dormer recess and then attach holdbacks in one of two ways: on the window frame ①, on the outer wall ②.

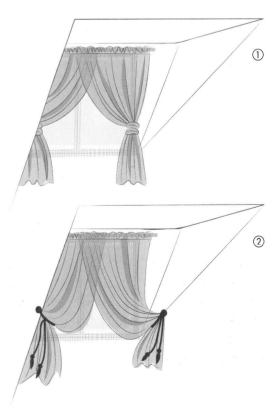

Delicate clips such as this gold-finish garland clip used on lace tiebacks will embellish the romantic style.

Rustic

Many of us yearn for an uncomplicated, peaceful, rural existence, where life can be slower and more meaningful, with fresh air to breathe and more room to move. That longing for an old-fashioned country lifestyle finds a rich expression in rustic style.

Wherever you live, it is possible to bring the earthy natural colours of the countryside right into your home by decorating with rustic style. While this look will always suit traditional architecture in a rural setting, be it grand country house, simple cottage or converted barn, it can easily be adapted for the modern townhouse in an urban setting too.

Rustic style is fresh, timeless and pretty – just like the countryside. The style favours simple and functional window treatments in basic fabrics with pretty trimmings, instead of more elaborate structured styles. Curtains are uncomplicated, with gathered, rod-pocket or pencil-pleat headings and can be short (to the windowsill) or long (to the floor). Blinds are as simple as a rolled stagecoach blind, or as basic as a Roman blind. Curtain rods with simple finials should be wooden, possibly with a distressed finish, or wrought iron.

As always, your choice of fabric is crucial in creating an authentic country look. Choose woven cotton or linen checks and stripes, including plaids for guaranteed country flavour, while printed florals, especially on glazed cotton chintz, and traditional toile de Jouy are both country perennials.

Mixing small-scale prints in a limited colour palette is a clever tip for creating a coordinated country look. Match a floral fabric with stripes or checks and one other small-scale pattern motif, such as a paisley. Follow this design and stick to only two colours, and you have the makings of classic rustic style.

Warm colours and soft textures epitomise comfortable rustic style in a country living room where long linen curtains with an unpleated heading hang from an innovative rod – a garden rake.

Casement windows

The informal casement window is perfect for dressing in a country style. In this bright panelled bedroom, fresh windowsill-length voile curtains with a pretty embroidered daisy motif and scalloped hem hang simply from a ruffled rod-pocket heading. This design retains privacy while still allowing light to flood in. When hanging lightweight sheers within the recess of a window frame, opt for a simple tension rod that is easy to install, and stays in place with an internal spring mechanism.

Headings can be kept simple for a country feel. A ruffled rod-pocket heading ①, a gathered heading ②, a plain rod-pocket heading ③.

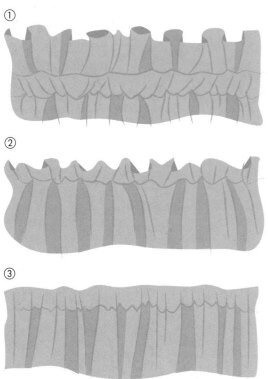

①

②

③

① ② ③

Fabrics that are lightweight and textured are ideal for a rustic style. Broderie Anglaise ①, a lace with daisy detail ②, a dragonfly-embroidered peach silk ③.

holders come in wood or metal, and they sometimes have a clip behind to hold the fabric in place. Antique rose effect ①, antique gold effect ②, cream gold effect ③.

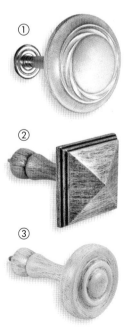

Ginghams and plaids are a great fabric choice for a rural feel. Here, a scarf has been made from a piece of red checked fabric with a contrasting lining and simply arranged over two carved wooden scarf holders painted to match the surrounding wall. A scarf without curtains makes a simple and stylish statement, but if more privacy is needed, a drop-down roller blind hidden behind the scarf can be added.

Corner windows

Stripes have been teamed with floral and plaid upholstery fabrics here – all key choices for a country-inspired interior. These fabrics would also work well. A smart grey/blue herringbone weave ticking ①, a blue check on a linen ground ②, a pale blue floral damask ③.

①

Windows on both sides of a corner can provide stunning views and the right treatment will frame these. In this country living room, the beamed ceiling and the black window frames have been reflected in the choice of curtain fabric. A bold, wide stripe in red, cream and black has been hung from black curtain rods with a simple pencil-pleat heading.

②

③

In other situations where two windows are close to a corner of a room, you may wish to unify them. Here, a double set of curtains perform this function very well. The plain curtains behind are of different lengths – one dropping to the floor, and one to a wide windowsill. The deeply pleated floral curtains in front are dress curtains only, and the pretty flowered tieback helps to divert the eye from the conflicting lengths behind.

Opt for curtain rods and holdbacks with elaborate cast-resin ram's head finials.

Sash windows

Tall sash windows have the best proportions for a dramatic dressing. Here, a bright and bold plaid fabric has been chosen for full-length curtains with an informal scarf arranged over a wooden rod. The tails almost reach down to the windowsill on either side, creating an eye-catching look that would not have been as effective on a shorter window with less elegant proportions.

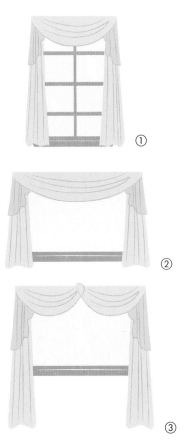

Successful swag and scarf treatments rely on attractive proportions. As a general rule, swags should be one fifth of the overall length of the curtains and tails should be two to three times longer than the swag. Sill-length curtains with a swag need short tails on a tall window ①, a single swag on a wide window needs shorter tails ②, a double swag on a wide window can carry longer tails ③.

Fabrics with pretty country prints are perfect for a rustic look. A bright strawberry print ①, an acorn and leaf print on linen ②, a floral chintz ③.

①

②

③

Curtain rods are made from various materials and offer many style choices. Traditional polished brass ①, stylish wood and metal combination ②, plain varnished wood ③.

①　　②　　③

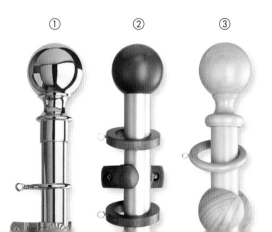

Curtains can be used to subtly alter the proportions of a room. In a high-ceilinged living room with a tall sash window, floral curtains with goblet-pleated headings hang from a rod that is much wider than the window. This gives the impression that the window is wider than it is, while showing off the fabric to its best advantage.

French windows

Combining different prints and limiting your colour scheme is a good way of achieving a rural, informal look. In this classic example, a fresh blue-and-white scheme creates a coordinated but informal rustic style. Wide French doors have been given a layered effect with a double set of curtains: one in a floral print bordered with a small check, and the lighter pair behind in a subtler print. With ruffled rod-pocket headings, both are held back from the centre with a pair of fabric tiebacks. The chairs and tablecloths are made up in other coordinating fabrics, including a stripe, for a cohesive but casual scheme.

Another way to combine more than one fabric is to use contrasting lining, which is revealed when the curtain is swept back with a high ruched tieback ①, a tented tieback ②.

①

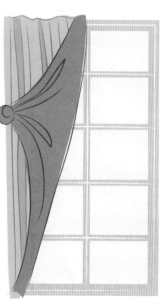

②

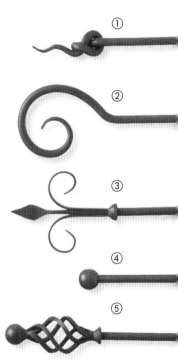

Narrow wrought-iron curtain rods with hand-forged finials in various designs. Knot finial ①, crook finial ②, fleur de lis finial ③, ball finial ④, basket finial ⑤.

French windows that open into a room rather than outside require a simple treatment with no valance or swag to obstruct the doors. Here, a wrought-iron rod with shepherd's crook finials is set above the elegant wide arch of the door, creating a sense of space and height. A striped fabric in a warm colour has been chosen for the simple, pleated curtains that frame the view onto a tranquil terrace.

①

②

③

Stripes are a classic country favourite. Choose a zigzag printed stripe ①, a textured woven wide stripe ②, a multi-coloured printed stripe on twill woven cotton ③.

Arched windows

Arched windows should be shown off, rather than concealed, so choose your treatment with care. This cabin has a magnificent set of arched windows, framing a spectacular mountain view. Honeycomb blinds in a neutral colour have been made to fit the individual shaped panes, while still leaving the structure of the window exposed. A motorised operating system for the blinds is essential for such high windows.

With such a large expanse of window, colour choice for window treatments is crucial. Blue will reflect the sky outside ①, a rusty red that matches the furnishings will draw the eye into the interior ②, a grey that matches the stonework is a neutral choice ③.

①

②

③

Opt for intricately carved or moulded curtain rods for a striking style statement. Cherrywood pole with ball finial ①, mahogany pole with gold-painted acorn finial ②, barley-twist mahogany pole with urn finial ③.

①

②

③

The toile de Jouy fabric featured in this room is a country classic. For alternatives, think of a rich wool paisley ①, a cut velvet leaf on a satin ground ②, a traditional floral print on a tea-stained linen ③.

Creating uniformity in your scheme will let the elegant structure of arched windows stand out. In an impressive but comfortable music room, the full-length curtains have been made in a printed design that closely matches the wallpaper, showing off the beautiful window. The curtain rod has been hung under the rafters above the window, leaving the arch exposed when the curtains are drawn during the day.

Picture windows

Very large windows are a focal point, but they can sometimes dominate a room. The effect of the huge picture window in this rustic dining room is minimised with a simple, unobtrusive blind to diffuse the light and maintain privacy.

Tall windows like this suit exaggerated or plain treatments. An asymmetrical swag ①, a deep swag with cascade tails ②, a plain heading ③.

Large picture windows grouped together let in plenty of light, but sometimes the light needs to be controlled. Here, it would be a shame to detract from the breathtaking panoramic mountain view. Accordingly, discreet vertical blinds in a translucent material have been hung across the full expanse of the window, allowing the view to be admired with the blinds closed as well as when they are open.

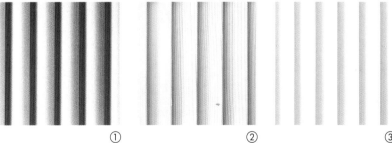

①   ②   ③

Vertical blinds provide a flexible system that combines precise light control with the advantage of a minimal stackback when they are opened. Choose from aluminium ①, wood ②, translucent vinyl ③.

Bay windows

  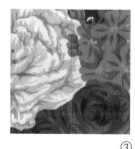

① ② ③

Traditional floral chintz is a key element of English country house style. A tulip print on fine cotton ①, a bird and flower print on white damask ②, a traditional floral chintz ③.

Bay windows tend to let in a lot of light and create a feeling of spaciousness. In the room pictured above, a wide bay window is given a traditional English country house treatment. Floral chintz has been used for three pairs of full-length curtains, which have serpentined valances (gathered valances shaped with more length over the curtain stackback area so that very little light is lost). The lower edge of the valance is softened with a pretty fan-edged fringing, while the top is defined with a rope-trimmed, ruched yoke.

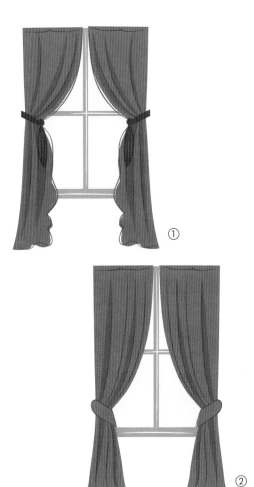

Tiebacks can be hung at various heights, but curtains should always be cut overly long so that they are not lifted too high off the ground when they are tied back. Rope tiebacks used at mid-window height ①, fabric-covered tiebacks used at windowsill height ②.

Bay window seats fit in well with a rustic look. In a cottage living room, curtains with a ruffled rod-pocket heading have been hung across the front of a bay window, leaving space to create a cosy window-seat area behind. The curtains are held back with jute tasselled tiebacks suspended from hooks that have been set high up on each side. This allows the curtains to be pulled out of the way and allow more light into the room. To enable the window seat to be used during the day and night, hang unobtrusive blinds close to the windows.

Jute and wood tassels have a rustic flair.

Doorways

Door curtains feature heavily in rustic style. Originally used to keep out cold draughts in older houses, they are now used to frame doorways, provide privacy on glass doors, and unify door and window treatments. On doors that open inwards, especially where there is little stackback room, a portiere rod that opens with the door can be used. This type of rod has the added benefit of closing with the door as you leave the house, providing around-the-clock draught control as well as security on glass doors. Here, a simple gingham is paired with pretty, spotted sheer fabric for a fresh and rustic style.

①   ②   ③

Use interlining to add insulating properties to door curtains, and to bulk out a multi-stripe cotton ticking ①, a bright red, white and blue plaid ②, a brushed denim with red pinstripe ③.

Portiere rods are hinged to open and close with the door. A bracket attached to the opening side of the door provides support for heavy curtains, while also allowing the rod to move with the door.

For an internal door that opens away from the curtains, or for an opening with no door at all, curtains can be hung from a rod built in above the doorway and drawn by hand. A printed silk has been heavily interlined to prevent cold draughts from travelling from the hallway into the cosy living room. A narrow metal rod with a distressed paint finish and glass ball finials are a delicate touch to complement the fabric.

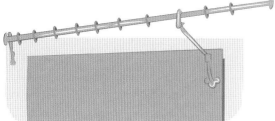

Some portiere rods feature a swivel arm bracket that raises the rod as the door opens, lifting the curtain so that it does not get stuck under the door. This means that curtains can be made to reach all of the way down to the floor, eliminating under-door draughts.

Problem windows

Very small windows can be difficult to dress, but rustic style lends itself to them. In this pretty bathroom, a tiny, plain window with a deep recess is given a simple and unobtrusive treatment with unlined, printed cotton, which has been hung close to the window within the recess to provide privacy and to gently filter the light. The curtains have deliberately been made with minimum fullness so that they do not appear too bulky and still leave room for ornaments and accessories to be displayed on the windowsill.

①　②　③

Coordinated prints in a limited colour palette are a good choice for small rooms and suit a rustic style. A black-on-white toile de Jouy print ①, a small-scale black floral print on white lawn ②, a white spot print on black sateen ③.

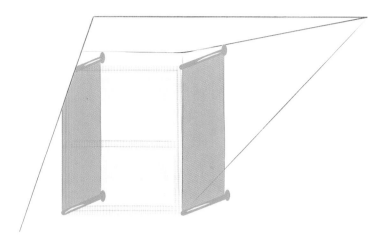

It is important not to obscure any light from a dormer window, but with so little room around the window frame, options are limited. Drapery arms are a classic solution. The brackets incorporate a hinge so that the rods can be pushed back to the walls on the sides of the dormer window during the day. At night they can be closed across the windows, with the tiebacks removed. In an attic bedroom, curtains with a rod-pocket heading on dormer rods are made from a checked fabric that matches the wallpaper and creates a unified, cosy atmosphere.

An unlined, lightweight panel can be held taut on drapery arms at the top and bottom to create a translucent type of shutter.

Retro

Retro comes from the word 'retrospective', which means 'to look back'. It is a contemporary term that is used to describe artefacts from a bygone 20th-century era – usually the interwar and postwar decades from the 1930s to the 1970s.

Retro style is defined by contemporary interiors' inclusion of original products such as car boot-sale finds of glassware and ceramics, as well as established designer originals in furniture, lighting and fabrics, such as those by Charles Eames or Mies van der Rohe.

Retro also refers to contemporary products that have been designed today, but have been inspired by yesterday. These include furniture, fabrics and accessories, but also a wide variety of items such as radios, refrigerators and so on, that are completely functionally up to date but have borrowed their styling features from a previous era.

When applying retro style to windows, the main element is, as always, the choice of fabric. There are a myriad of fabric designs available

that range from reproductions of classic vintage designs, such as 1930s Art Deco moquette upholstery fabric or 1950s Hawaiian prints, through to modern interpretations of vintage themes, such as those by the Finnish design company Marimekko. Alternatively, if you want to keep the windows understated, there are still plenty of options that will not detract from the period look.

Look for contemporary accessories with a vintage feel, such as today's stainless-steel curtain rods with cool 1960s-inspired finials, or slinky tasselled tiebacks that hint at 1930s Hollywood. Or sometimes just opting for a vintage colour scheme such as 1950s pastel shades or 1970s purples may be all that is necessary to capture the spirit of retro style.

Wooden Venetian blinds always conjure up a 1940s Chandleresque era.

Picture windows

Clever positioning of a curtain rod or track can balance the proportions of a wide picture window. Here, the rod has been hung in the dead space above the window, halfway between the top of the window and the ceiling. An undulating eyelet heading shows off a vintage 1950s fabric with an oversize print to a great effect.

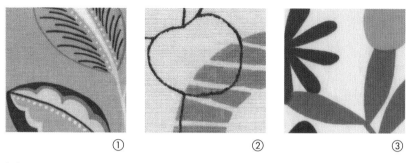

① ② ③

Many contemporary printed fabrics favour retro designs such as this 1950s-inspired leaf design in brown and cream on aqua linen ①, a 1950s-style abstract print on white linen ②, a bright 1960s-style floral print on white cotton ③.

Choose 1950s-inspired shapes for finials. Bronze glass tablet finial ①, maple baton finial ②, frosted slice finial ③.

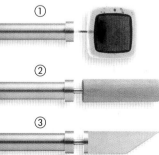

①
②
③

Wide and tall picture windows offer fantastic views, but they will also allow heat to build up and allow in damaging UV light. In order to insulate this living room against the heat and to protect the furnishings, light-filtering woven wood blinds offer maximum protection and add sharp detailing to this retro-inspired setting.

Hang a fabric-topped dressing over Venetian blinds to hide the mechanism and add some vintage flair. A gathered valance made with 1950s-style fabric ①, a box pelmet covered with 1950s-style fabric ②.

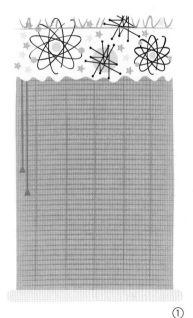

①

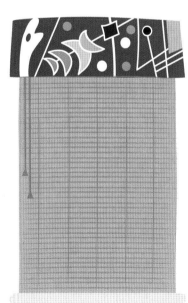

②

Corner windows

Complement

a 1960s interior
with bright brass
contemporary rods
with stylish glass finials.
Turquoise crystal ball
①, green glass ball ②,
frosted amber ball ③.

Echo the window dressing style of your chosen period to create an authentic retro interior. Curtains were fairly minimalist during the 1960s, and these plain, lightweight cotton curtains, in a 1960s shade of orange, are the perfect example. Two slender rods have been hung above the large windows in the corner of a room, with a single curtain hanging on each rod. This means that, when they are open, the corner is clear, unifying the two windows.

Choose plain woven cotton in colours from a 1960s palette. Aqua blue ①, sunshine yellow ②, burnt orange ③.

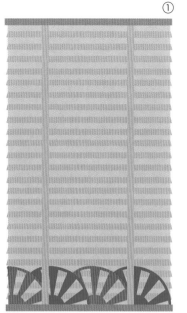

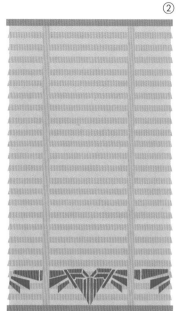

Add a 1930s touch to wooden Venetian blinds by stencilling a graphic Art Deco border of a fan design ①, a geometric pattern ②.

Venetian blinds are a good choice for two windows that are so close to a corner that space would be limited for a pair of voluminous curtains. Here, in this 1930s-inspired room, dark wooden blinds add to the sophistication of the muted colours, surface textures and elegant styling, casting moody shadows across the room.

Casement windows

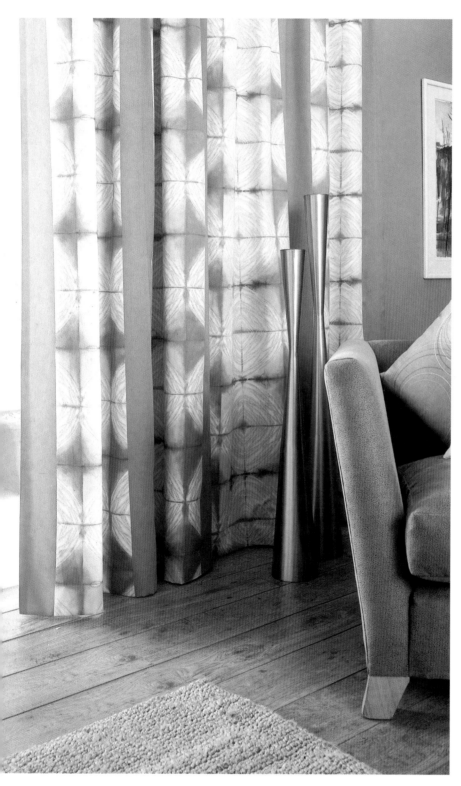

The interior fashions of a past era can be adapted with ease for modern tastes. Here, vertical bands in a plain blue have been added at regular intervals to some 1960s-style tie-dye curtains. This helps to break up the busy pattern and draw attention to the overall height of the room. The subtle choice of colour, instead of the more unrestrained colours that were typical of the 1960s, helps to make this fabric work in a modern setting.

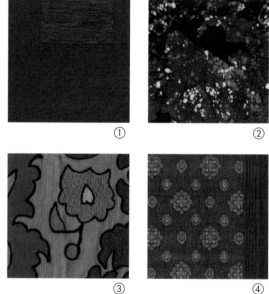

①   ②

③   ④

Subtler window treatments with a 1960s feel could feature a shimmering double-cloth with square motifs ①, a spattered batik design ②, an abstract embroidered crewelwork design ③, a crinkle-pleated fabric with Indian-style borders ④.

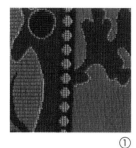

①

②

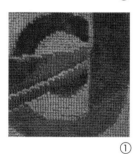

①

Textiles in the
1950s were influenced
by the abstract art of the
period. A woven abstract
design in rich colours ①,
a monochrome velvet
with a diamond motif ②,
a tapestry weave with
abstract pattern ③.

Short, windowsill-length curtains were the norm in mid-20th-century interiors,
when practical modernism was still linked to the frugality of the interwar years.
These curtains in an exuberant abstract print are a perfect interpretation of
vintage 1950s style, stopping at the windowsill. A woven wood blind hangs
behind the curtains to provide privacy and light control and also blends well with
the wooden furniture in the room.

Sash windows

When windows have a deep recessed architrave it's appropriate to fit blinds inside the recess, positioning them close to the glass so that the surrounding frame is exposed. Here on these sash windows, roller blinds are a timeless choice that will not detract from the 1970s feel of this kitchen/diner. They are also practical for kitchens since they do not trap dirt and dust, will roll right up out of the way if necessary, and are available in stain-resistant fabric that can be cleaned.

①

②

For a less restrained style, look for vintage prints on roller blinds. Handbags and heels print ①, a kaleidoscopic pattern ②.

Colour-coordinated floral fabrics and wallpaper in a limited colour palette will provide a cohesive and, ultimately, restful decorating scheme. This bedroom is a modern interpretation of early-20th-century interiors, with its use of traditional furniture and styling. Full-length curtains with pinch-pleat headings are hung from a traditional painted wooden rod that has been hung across the top of the window, very close to the ceiling.

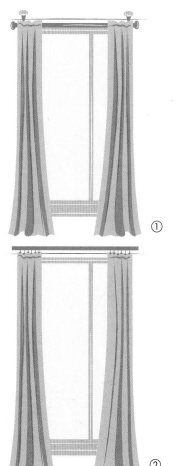

①

②

① ② ③

Mixing patterns from a limited colour range creates a harmonious scheme. A delicate trailing-leaf pattern ①, a Jacquard woven-leaf design ②, a floral tapestry weave ③.

When a window reaches almost all of the way to the ceiling, occasionally there is no room for a rod, especially if there is cornicing around the ceiling. Rods can be hung from the ceiling ①, a track can be attached to the ceiling ②.

Sliding doors

The central division in a wide sliding window is sometimes an ugly feature. In this stylish 1970s-inspired living room, a double-pole system supports a pair of functional eyelet-headed curtains in front of a set of striped banners. The central banner neatly hides the sliding window frame and serves to break up the wide expanse of the window. Fabrics have been chosen in a colourway that is redolent of the later 1960s and 1970s to complement and coordinate with the other vintage elements in the room, such as the glassware and lighting.

Choosing a colour scheme that echoes a vintage period is a great way to unify a retro look. Psychedelic oranges and pinks ①, black-and-white Pop Art ②, 1970s oranges ③.

①

②

③

Flat panels can help to frame a large sliding door. Here, panels with a deep slotted heading hang from a contemporary steel rod, with glass finials. The fabric choice is pure vintage 1960s – an outrageous floral print. The essential factor is to choose two slightly differing colours for each panel – one on a dark ground colour, and the other on a light ground colour – for an unexpected, off-key twist.

① ② ③ ④

Bright floral prints were typical of the 1960s. A multi-coloured floral print on white cotton ①, a large-scale blue petal print on white cotton ②, a daisy design in orange and beige ③, a stylised flower in dark orange flock on a linen ground ④.

Bay windows

Bay windows present a great opportunity for installing window seating. In order to provide privacy at all times of the day, while still using the seating, functional short curtains or blinds have to be hung within the bay window itself. Full-length curtains such as these that hang from a pole fitted across the front of the bay are purely dress curtains used to soften the look and add elegance. The retro look is created with a fabric choice in a monochrome colourway and print that is reminiscent of the 1960s.

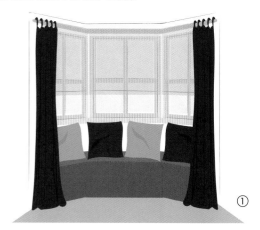

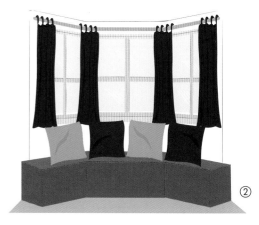

Window seats in a bay present a problem when it comes to choosing treatments. Consider full-length dress curtains with blinds close to the windows ①, short sill-length curtains close to the windows ②.

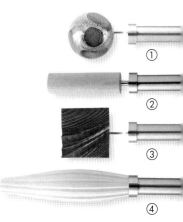

Choose from the following finials to complement this kind of interior. Floating glass ball finial ①, maple baton finial ②, square ripple cutout finial ③, maple bullet finial ④.

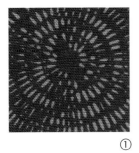

①   ②   ③

A beautiful and imposing trio of arched windows in a deep bay with elaborate plaster cornicing provide a wonderful opportunity to use swathes of fabric for both face curtains and sheer curtains. A flamboyant retro print that evokes the 1960s and 1970s has been chosen to provide a sharp, stylish contrast to the traditional features of the architecture.

Bold medallion prints are an echo of the 1960s and 1970s. An abstract circular motif printed on linen union ①, large and small dots in a shimmering manmade fibre ②, a tapestry weave with large daisies ③.

Global

Since humans first began to circumnavigate the globe and trade with other cultures centuries ago, artefacts and textiles have travelled with them, influencing design and style at home. Now, with the amazing variety of global furniture, fabrics and art available to us, either on our travels or in a store much nearer to home, it is easier than ever before to furnish our lives with global ingredients and exotic influences.

Choosing a window treatment to achieve a global style might be as simple as selecting a practical roller blind to create an impression of Japanese simplicity and minimalism, or a wooden Venetian blind to imply the natural earthiness of Africa. However, it is also tempting to use exotic textiles such as the beautiful wax resist batiks of Indonesia to create curtains. Other fabrics exude more traditional styles from around the world. A floral chintz is typical of the English countryside, while Provençal prints are synonymous with the south of France.

Colour is also an important ingredient of global style – a vivid blue with white will instantly evoke the Greek islands, while vibrant pinks and oranges transport us to the Indian subcontinent. Accessories and trimmings provide hints of far-flung shores, too. A tabbed curtain hung on a simple bamboo pole and trimmed with a delicate mother-of-pearl beaded fringe could transport you to a South Sea island. Wrought-iron rods have an obvious Spanish flavour, while exotic tasselled tiebacks can bring to mind the plains of Africa.

Whether you want to base your scheme on a specific region or simply allude to far-off places, incorporating global influences will create an interior that is undeniably unique.

Unlined gauzy white voile has been tied onto wooden curtain rods in generous folds to filter the light and complement the southeast Asian flavour of the furniture in this exotic bedroom.

Sash windows

Curtain rods with an antique brass finish are a sophisticated choice. A barley-twist pole and urn finial ①, a reeded pole and acorn finial ②, a plain pole with ball finial ③.

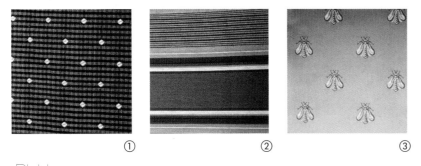

①   ②   ③

Use dark colours and richly textured fabrics to create an opulent, cosmopolitan style. A pair of sash windows is treated as one in this example, where heavy curtains with a deep rod-pocket heading hang from a substantial wooden rod, held back with elaborately tasselled tiebacks hung from wooden holdbacks.

Richly textured weaves are ideal for this opulent style. A dark blue woven check with embroidered dot ①, a richly coloured woven stripe ②, a gold satin with embroidered bee motif ③.

For alternatives to wooden Venetian blinds, choose a woven wood Roman blind ①, a rolled-up split bamboo blind ②.

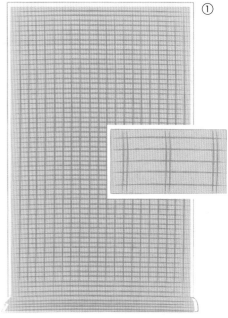

①

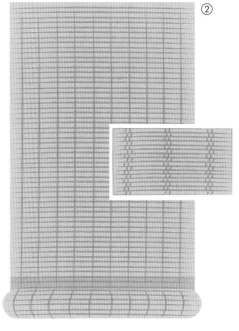

②

Wooden Venetian blinds capture the beauty of real wood and come in a variety of natural wood and painted finishes. A good tip is to choose a finish that blends in to the window frame as closely as possible to provide a cohesive look. Tribal artefacts and natural textures bring a North African flavour to this room, and coordinate with the wooden blind.

Casement windows

Some global looks are simple to recreate. For Greek island style choose the quintessentially Greek combination of blue and white, pare the structure down to painted brickwork, tile floors and beamed ceilings, and add soft blue and white, or white on white, furnishings. For windows, use unlined white curtains with simple gathered headings and a deep frill at the top, hung from painted wooden rods. If, as here, the casements open inwards, make sure the curtains can pull far enough back off the windows.

Handpainted wooden curtain rods with delicately carved finials can bring to mind faraway places. A fluted pole with obelisk end, painted white with cloud-blue highlights ①, a reeded pole with acorn end, painted midnight blue with gold highlights ②, a plain pole with Arabic end, painted cream with purple highlights ③, a fluted pole and fluted ball, painted with soft ivory and blue highlights ④.

To shade a bright window in a sophisticated European style, use a dark spotted sheer fabric paired with a luxurious textured flock print. Curtains in both fabrics have been slotted as one onto a chrome rod, creating deep uniform folds of fabric that match the neat symmetry of the setting. The stained-glass top windowpane is always visible through the sheer curtain.

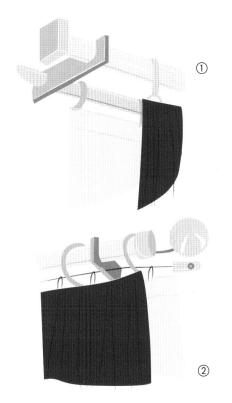

To enable two sets of curtains to function independently, choose a double-pole system ①, a pole-and-wire system ②.

Stylish fabrics with surface texture and sheen will give a glamorous look. A dark gold silk and cotton double cloth with large woven-leaf pattern ①, an embossed black on turquoise damask ②, a smart black and magenta stripe ③.

①

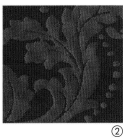
②

③

Bay windows

Bays often consist of several windows and a window treatment can help to unify them. Here, three windows in a deep square recess or bay are each dressed in a fabric blind in a Far Eastern-style fabric, while a pair of full-length curtains hangs across the front of the bay to blend them all together. Vertical-striped patterns and borders are always a good choice for blinds, partially because they are displayed flat so that their impact is not lost within folds of fabric. Any folds in a blind are usually horizontal, as in a pleated Roman blind, and leave the pattern virtually uninterrupted.

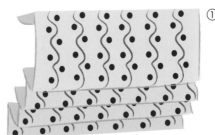

①

②

Horizontal folds found in a Roman blind enhance the impact of vertical stripes. A delicate stripe ①, a bold stripe ②.

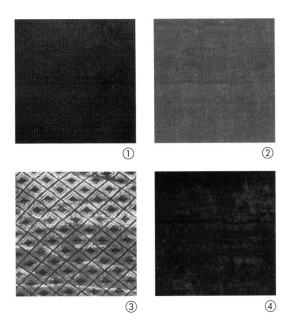

① ② ③ ④

Brightly coloured textiles with glitter and shine bring the East closer to home. A red dupioni silk ①, a tangerine cotton voile ②, an orange and gold geometric weave ③, a deep purple sheer ④.

Bring the look of a casbah right into your home with gauzy layers of sheer fabric, filtering the light into a desert haze. Hanging double layers of sheer fabrics in differing colours creates interesting combinations of vibrant hues as one overlaps another. Here, a blind has been hung behind the sheer curtains. For a more exotic touch, add a shaped bottom edge to the blind, perhaps with a beaded trim.

Picture windows

Global style allows for less formal window treatments. In a casual, south of the border style, curtains with an abstract print are suspended from a wire across a wall-to-wall window with a fabulous coastal view. Wires are a minimal way to suspend curtains, but they can only carry very lightweight fabric.

① ②

Draw rods are attached to the leading ring of a curtain and can help draw back curtains with more ease and protect the fabric from being handled.

Rough outlines on these linen prints give a hand-drawn quality. A leaf design ①, an abstract pattern ②, a rough stripe ③.

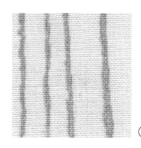

③

Blinds in a semi-opaque fabric will let in plenty of light even when lowered. The floor-to-ceiling wooden framed windows in this Japanese-influenced kitchen are each fitted with a Roman blind that allows light to filter in. When total light elimination is not essential, hanging the blinds lower than the top of the window allows a view of the outside world while still maintaining privacy, but crucially, as here, it also unifies the differing heights of two sets of windows.

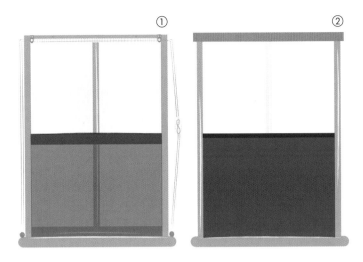

Ingenious roller blinds offer privacy on the lower part of the window, but let light in at the top. A bottom-up roller blind is fitted at sill level and rolls upwards ①, a roller blind made of a panel of opaque fabric at the base and white mesh at the top ②.

French windows

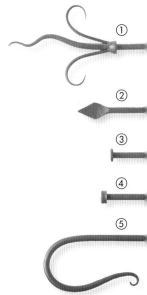

Slender steel rods with forged finials suit the graphic prints on display. Fleur de lis finial ①, arrowhead finial ②, flat-end cap finial ③, stud end finial ④ crook finial ⑤.

Fabric choice is crucial for an ethnic look. For inspiration, look at sarongs, pareus and saris. In this room, French windows are dressed with one curtain panel hanging from a slender metal rod. The dark wood floor and furniture are complemented by a collection of ethnic textiles on display in this room, creating an atmosphere that evokes the Far East.

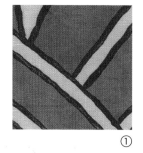

①

②

③

Ethnic prints and textured sheers are key fabric choices that evoke far-off places. An earthy block print on rough textured cotton ①, a block-printed stripe ②, a rough textured open-weave sheer ③.

①

②

③

Venetian blinds are very versatile. In this room, the windows have been given a simple treatment with wooden blinds. Notice how individual blinds have been hung on each door of these inward-opening French windows, while the transom above has one blind across the entire width. The blinds have been stained dark to match the hardwood floor of this room, which looks like it has come straight out of Africa, with its huge, metal-framed four-poster bed swathed in simple white cotton.

Colour choice is crucial for introducing an exotic flavour into your home. White paintwork contrasts with an ebony floor to evoke Africa ①, deep blues and earthy terracotta are reminiscent of the Mediterranean ②, natural hues bring to mind the Far East ③.

Problem windows

In a bathroom, window treatments need to withstand dirt and steam. For windows that are very close to the bathtub or shower, as here, materials that are water-, stain-, and mould-resistant are essential, so blinds in a tough, manmade fabric are a good choice. Another top priority in a bathroom is privacy, which is why these bottom-up blinds are such a good idea. They can be raised as high as is necessary for privacy, while still offering a constant view of the outside world at the top. And in a Japanese-inspired bathroom like this, the sleek, minimalist lines of the blinds suit the setting perfectly.

Versatile blinds that can be raised and lowered from bottom up or top down give ultimate control. Raise the blind so that the lower portion of window is open to reveal the view ①, lower the blind for privacy ②.

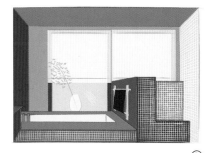

①

②

Tieback hooks and curtain clips can be imaginatively used to hang up lightweight curtains.

①

②

③

Crisp silk organzas in vibrant colours are perfect for global style. A multi-coloured organza stripe ①, a tangerine and pink spot organza ②, a subtle rose-patterned organza ③.

Some global styles suit a more casual, homemade look. In an unusual bathroom, an entirely different, eclectic approach with an Indian theme has been taken, with stunning, embroidered sari fabrics hung loosely. Light filters through the diaphanous fabric in the window, while panels of extra fabric provide further screening within the room, creating an oasis of exotic style.

Children's

Decorating children's rooms presents a wonderful opportunity to let your imagination run wild. Bright colours and bold imagery are used to create many of the fantastic children's furnishings available today, so it is possible to tailor a room to suit your child's age and personality. You may prefer to choose simple fabrics such as plain materials, stripes and checks that can be used together in either pastel or primary colours to great effect in a child's room.

First, you need to decide whether you want to create a vibrant, stimulating environment where your child will play, or a peaceful haven that will help soothe your child to sleep. If sleep is the goal, as is the case with babies and young toddlers, then close attention must be paid to eliminating as much light as possible from the room. For total blackout, especially during daylight hours, you will need to hang a blind made of blackout fabric close to the window, followed by blackout-lined curtains. Make sure that the curtains return to the wall on either side of the window to stop light leaking in from the sides. Then dress the top with a blackout-lined valance or pelmet that will stop light from reflecting across the ceiling.

Pay attention to safety factors as well. Dangling cords are a great temptation and a possible danger to an inquisitive child, so avoid them or keep them out of reach. Attach tiebacks higher than normal, and avoid overly long curtains that will get in the way.

Finally, remember that children grow and develop quickly, so leave room to adapt and alter the style as this happens. Teddy-bear prints will soon be outgrown, so use them on bedding and cushions that can be changed more easily than window treatments.

Pretty pink pleated Roman blinds cover a trio of nursery windows under a cheerful red zigzag pelmet.

Casement windows

Where space is limited, blinds may be a better solution than curtains. In this bedroom, roller blinds in a vivid, graphic-printed cotton coordinate with the cushions and bedding. For roller blinds like these, choose a bright print and have it laminated with a blackout backing to eliminate all light. Remember to ask for the blind to be reverse rolled – meaning that the fabric rolls over the top of the tube – otherwise you will see the reverse of the fabric on the tube.

① ②

③ ④

Prints for kids are always fun. A cotton candy stripe ①, a retro-style print of little girls and puppies ②, a pink batik-style floral ③, a delicate butterfly print ④.

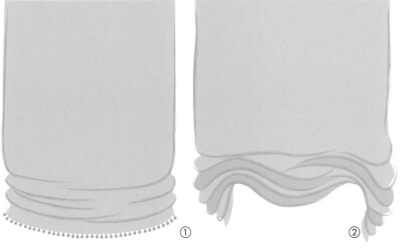

Less minimal blinds may obscure more light, but add a softer touch. A lightly pleated Roman blind with side ties and tassel trim ①, a cascade blind ②.

① ②

If a window has shutters, careful thought must be given to additional window treatments. In this pretty pink nursery, interlined gingham curtains have been hung from a bow-shaped board with a deep goblet heading, and Italian stringing has been used to hold the curtains level with the top of the shutters. The board not only makes an attractive shape as the curtains curve gracefully into the room, it also ensures that there is plenty of room for the shutters to fold back without being obstructed by the curtains.

For an alternative method of creating a bowed curtain, choose a sleekly curved stainless-steel rod.

Picture windows

Light control is very important in a nursery. Here, on wide picture windows, versatile blinds that combine tilting vanes are suspended inside two layers of sheer fabric to diffuse light when the vanes are open and to provide additional shading from the sun's rays when the vanes are tilted. The tops of the full-length plaid curtains are covered with wooden cornice boxes, which will ensure that all light is blocked out while the baby sleeps.

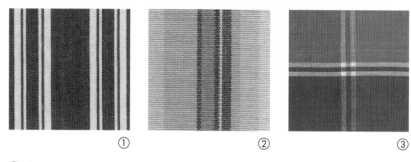

①   ②   ③

Stripes and checks are a great choice for children's rooms. A bright red ticking stripe ①, a multi-coloured woven stripe ②, a blue-and-white plaid ③.

For an older child, blocking out the light may not be as crucial. In this bedroom, an attractive pink floral print has been made into an unlined, unpleated curtain with a tab heading that hangs down from a narrow steel rod, allowing light to gently diffuse through the fabric. However, if light is a problem, a discreet roller blind in a blackout fabric hung within the window's recess will do the job.

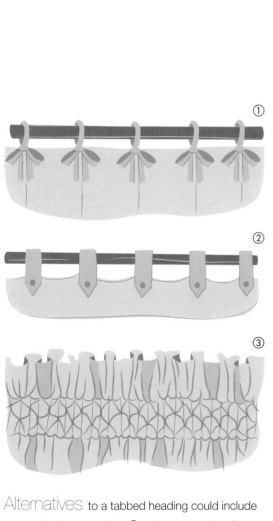

Alternatives to a tabbed heading could include a bow-tied loop heading ①, a button tab heading ②, a smocked heading with ruffle ③.

French windows

Blue and white is a classic colour combination for children's rooms – especially when accented with red. A fresh blue-and-white plaid ①, a blue, red and cream check ②, a multi-stripe in various shades of blue with bright red ③.

①

②

③

Colour choice is key when decorating children's rooms. Full-length curtains in an oversize blue-and-white gingham hang in large French windows in this sunny nursery. These colours are a great choice for children's rooms as, unlike with more gender- and age-specific designs, they'll never grow out of such a classic combination. Here the blue-and-white theme is accented to great effect with a tiny dash of red – a simple ribbon that ties the curtains back high up and out of the reach of young children.

Stagecoach blinds are the simplest type of blind, but they are not designed to be pulled up and down easily.

If a French window opens outwards and, consequently, there is no problem with obstructing the door, blinds are a possibility. Here a busy fabric has been made into a deeply scooped cascade blind hanging within the recess of a tall, narrow French window. Blinds like this have to be arranged carefully when they are pulled up, so it can pay to pair them with another roller blind behind, which can be pulled down for instant privacy and light control.

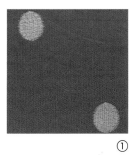

①

②

③

Sophisticated teenagers will love bright and jazzy prints. An embroidered multi-coloured spot on hot pink cotton ①, a wavy print with metallic highlights ②, a vivid floral print ③.

Corner windows

Light, heat and privacy control are important considerations in a child's room – especially one with this many windows. These versatile blinds feature two separate fabric panels, one translucent and one opaque. A clever top-down or bottom-up opening mechanism, which, when combined, provides limitless options for controlling conditions within the room – from filtering out glare to a total night-time blackout.

Choosing the right colour scheme is important in children's rooms. Pale pink for girls ①, red, white and blue is always popular ②, yellows and greens are restful ③.

①

②

③

Twisted rope tiebacks come in brilliant colours. Apricot ①, sienna ②, Wedgwood blue ③, barley ④, jade ⑤.

In this nursery, clever décor has been used to help separate two corner windows and create a sense of space. By painting the walls in two contrasting primary colours, the corner where the colours meet is strongly delineated and the two windows are clearly separated. In this busy, colourful room, patterned curtains would have been overpowering. Instead, two pairs of plain curtains in a deep blue fabric with bright red rope tiebacks contrast with the surrounding wall colours.

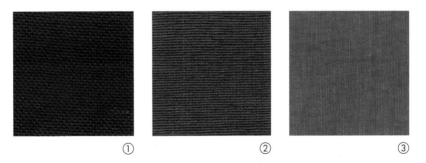

Plain fabrics for curtains add blocks of primary colour to a child's room. A chunky woven cotton comes in ruby red ①, marine blue ②, soothing green ③.

Sash windows

① ② ③

Gingham checks will always suit a child's room. A small-scale red gingham ①, a powder-blue gingham ②, a pale pink gingham ③.

Children's rooms should always be light and bright. To allow plenty of light into this pretty bedroom, a pair of sash windows is treated as one window. This effect is created by using a ruffle-headed valance over full-length cream cotton curtains bordered with a wide band of pink gingham on both the leading edge and the hem. Notice how the valance has been set at ceiling height, which fills the dead space above the window.

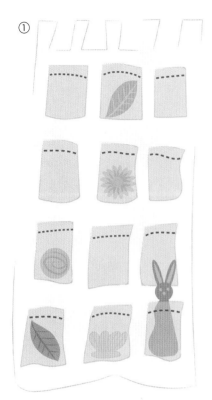

Try a novel idea that will entrance children and even help them clean up their rooms at the end of the day: Construct a patchwork of vibrantly coloured cotton that is large enough to make into a full-length curtain. Add large pockets near the bottom of the curtain so that small children can have fun putting their toys away.

Giving the curtains in a child's room another purpose can be both fun and useful. An organza panel with pockets for storing pictures, dried flowers or shells ①, a felt curtain with letters and pictures attached with Velcro ②.

Problem windows

Skylights are a great way to flood a room with light, but it is important to be able to control both light and heat when you want to. The best way to cover a skylight is with blinds that have been especially made for the purpose. Available in pleated or roller versions in a variety of opacities from sheer to blackout, they fit behind runners down the side of the skylight frame, holding them in place and sealing out any light leakage.

Other ingenious ways of covering skylights use cords to keep the fabric close to the window. A panel held back by ropes and rings ①, a Roman blind that runs down cords that have been attached to the wall on either side of the window ②.

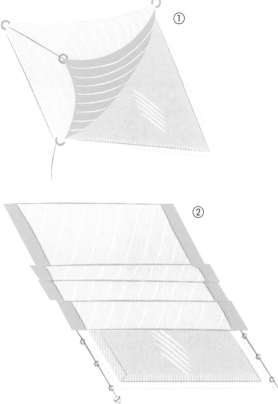

Sloping walls situated next to windows can restrict the options for window treatments. This awkward arched window is so close to a sloped ceiling that hardly any room is left for a curtain. A rod has been hung as far across as is possible, while interlined curtains in a bright space-age print distract the eye from the cramped spacing.

Finished off by a glass ball finial with blue LED lighting, this rod makes a funky addition to the room.

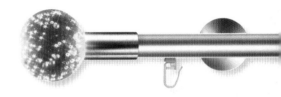

① ②

③

Pictorial prints that appeal to boys could include a vintage 1950s cowboy print ①, a hot-air balloon printed cotton ②, a space-age stars and rockets print ③.

Headings

A curtain heading has two functions. The main function is to provide a means of attaching the curtain to its supporting track or rod, either with the help of hooks that are inserted behind the heading, or by the heading itself, in the case of tabs, loops or eyelets. The secondary function is to provide fullness to the fabric, usually by pleating or gathering. The fullness is either set, as it is with a handmade French-pleated heading, or adjustable, by pulling up the cords of a readymade heading tape.

Plain rod pocket

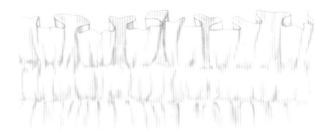

Ruffled rod pocket

Gathered

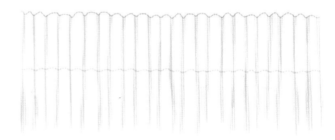

Pencil pleat

Goblet pleat

Smocked

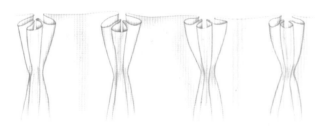

French, or triple, pleat

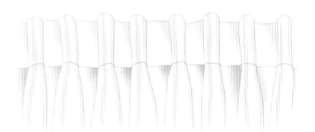

Cartridge pleat

Flat curtain-ring heading

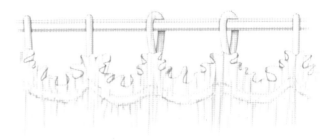

Curtain-ring heading with ruffle

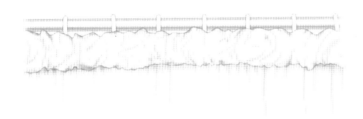

Curtain-ring heading with puff

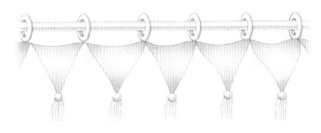

Curtain-ring heading with pennant foldover

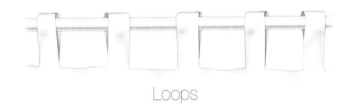

Loops

Tabs

Loops with deep scallops

Bow-tied loops

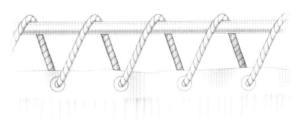

Eyelet

Eyelet with rope loops

Valances

Valances are a soft, fabric treatment used to dress the top of a window. Primarily used to hide the curtains' hardware and the top of the window frame, valances can be used to alter the proportions of a window or to unify windows of different shapes or sizes within the same room. They may also, of course, be purely decorative, adding volume, flair and detail to your window treatment.

Tented

Ribbon and eyelet

Stepped inverted box pleat

Tabbed

Teardrop

Crenellated

Banner

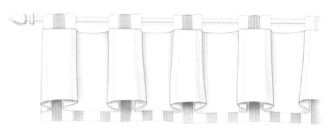

Inverted box pleat with tabs

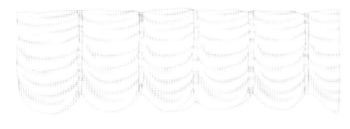

Austrian

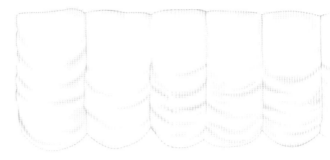

Balloon

Cloud with rod pocket

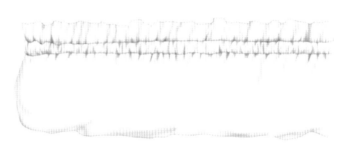

Puff

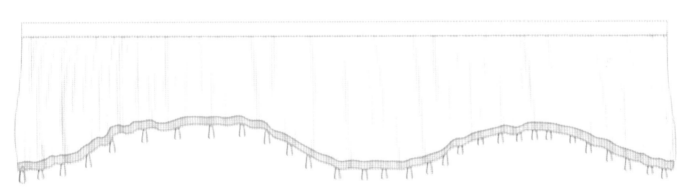

Gathered with braiding and tassels

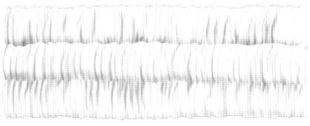

Triple rod pocket

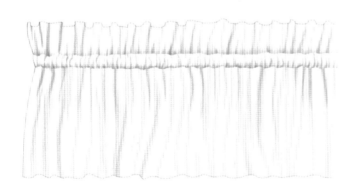

Gathered with rod pocket and ruffle

Bell pleat

Cornices and pelmets

Like valances, cornices and pelmets are a window-top treatment for a curtain arrangement, used to hide hardware, alter proportions, or unify windows of varying sizes within the same room. Unlike valances, cornices and pelmets are made of wood or other stiff materials. Cornices can be painted and embellished with moulding, and pelmets are usually upholstered with fabric. In some instances they also form a visible support for valances or swags.

Traditionally shaped wooden cornice

Beehive cornice

Box pelmet covered
with pleated fabric

Pennant pelmet

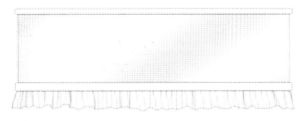

Box cornice with ruffle

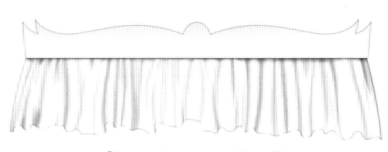

Shaped cornice with ruffle

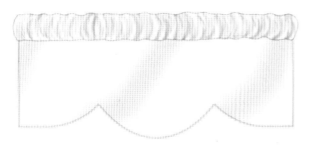

Scalloped cornice with shirred band

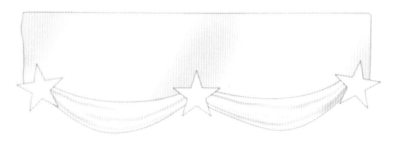

Scalloped pelmet with gathered
drapery and star details

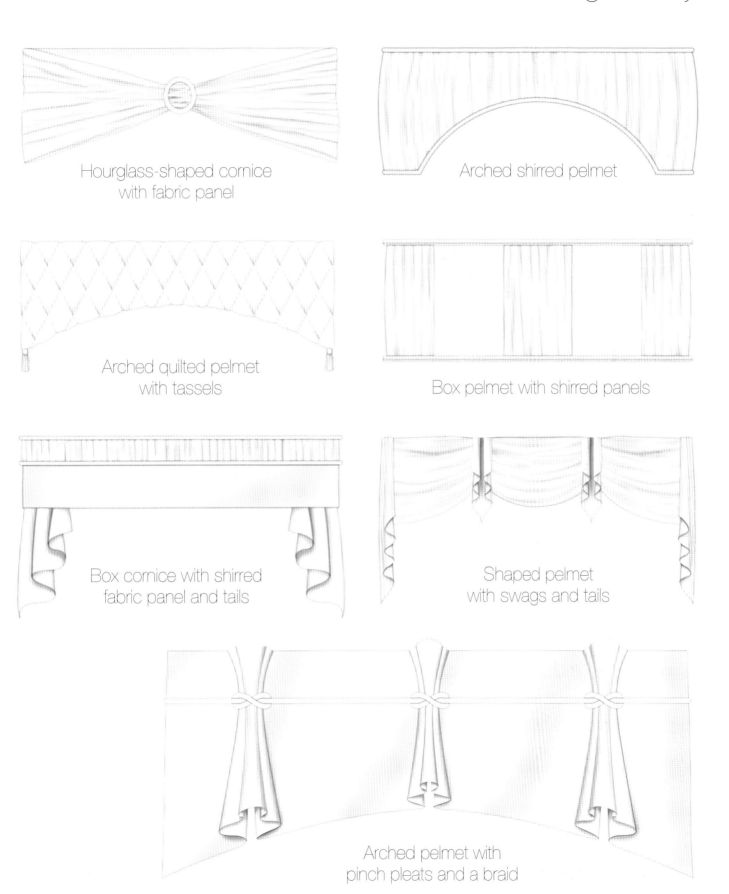

Hourglass-shaped cornice
with fabric panel

Arched shirred pelmet

Arched quilted pelmet
with tassels

Box pelmet with shirred panels

Box cornice with shirred
fabric panel and tails

Shaped pelmet
with swags and tails

Arched pelmet with
pinch pleats and a braid

Lambrequins

Lambrequins are similar to cornices, but they also reach at least two-thirds of the way down the sides of a window. Often elaborately shaped, upholstered with fabric and richly adorned with trim, their purpose is to embellish the shape of a plain window, drawing the eye into the room instead of out by adding opulence and style to a decorating scheme.

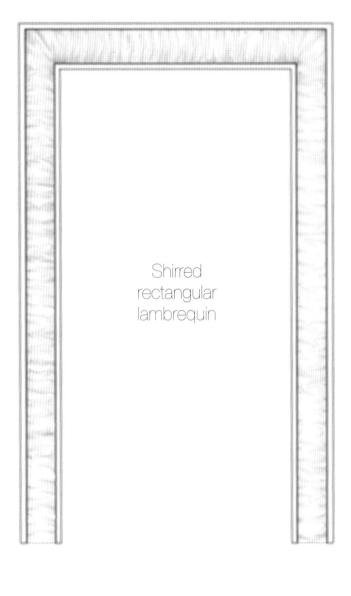

Shirred rectangular lambrequin

Shaped lambrequin with welt edge

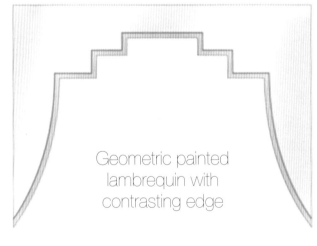

Geometric painted lambrequin with contrasting edge

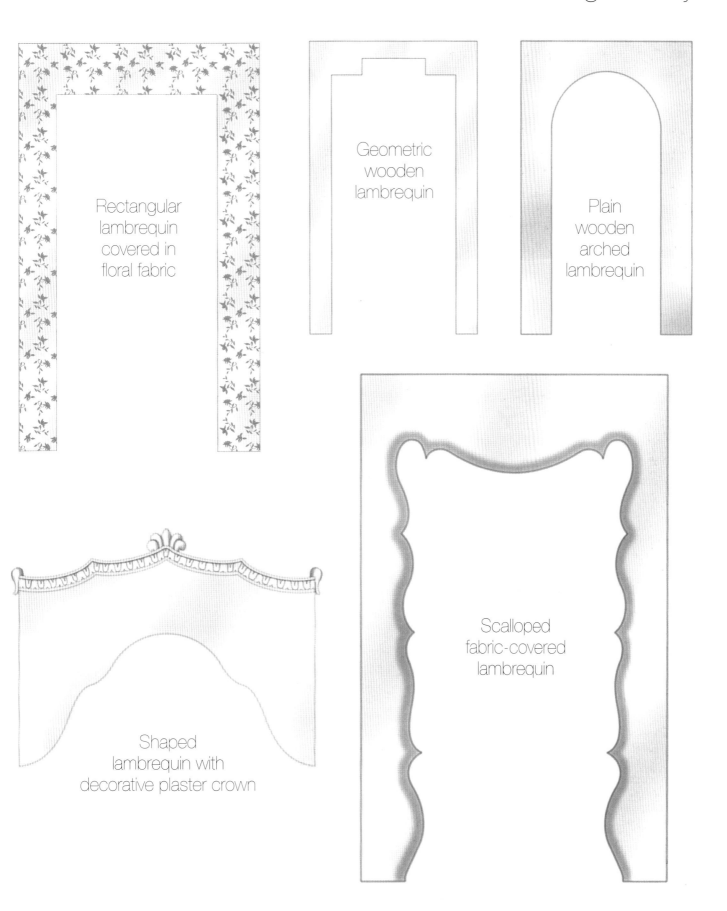

Rectangular lambrequin covered in floral fabric

Geometric wooden lambrequin

Plain wooden arched lambrequin

Shaped lambrequin with decorative plaster crown

Scalloped fabric-covered lambrequin

Scarves

Less tailored than swags and tails, scarves are an informal and romantic way of dressing the top of a window arrangement. Usually made from lightweight – even sheer – fabrics, scarves are supported by a rod or ornamental brackets and decoratively draped or wrapped across a window, sometimes ending in tails on one or both sides.

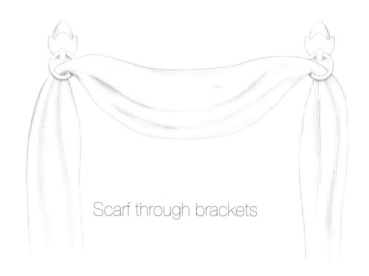

Scarf through brackets

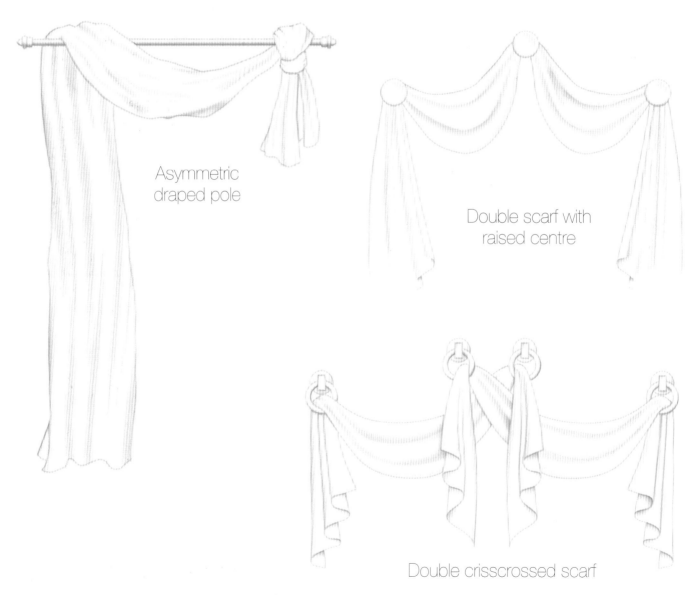

Asymmetric
draped pole

Double scarf with
raised centre

Double crisscrossed scarf

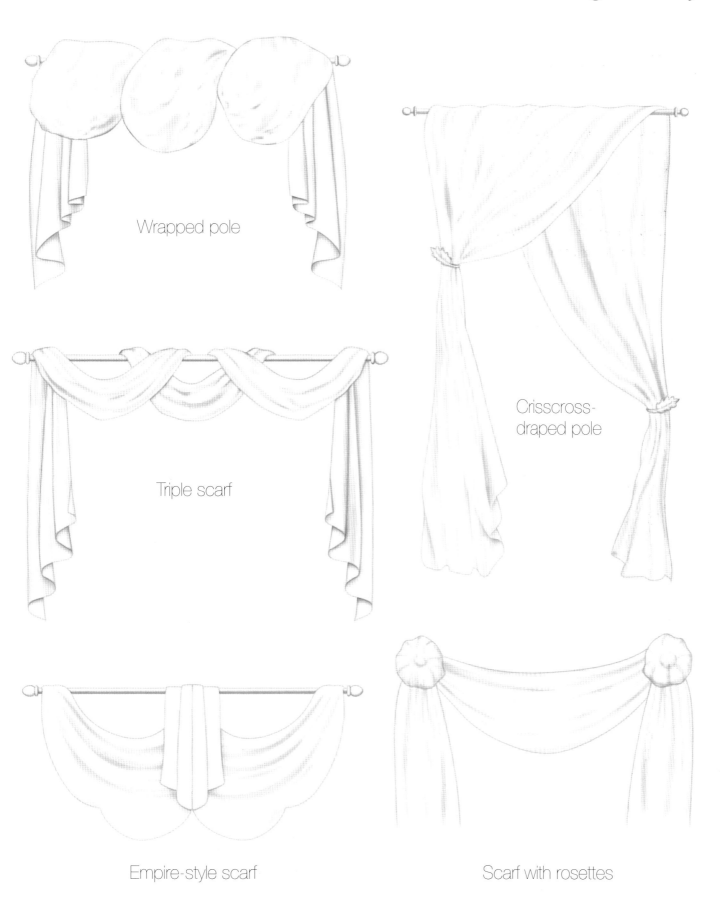

Wrapped pole

Triple scarf

Crisscross-
draped pole

Empire-style scarf

Scarf with rosettes

Swags

Usually suspended from a board or curtain rod across the top of a window, swags are elaborately pleated to form the fabric into tailored scoops and are usually paired with pleated tails on both sides. Often embellished with braiding or a fringe along the bottom edge, swags provide grandeur and opulence to a formal curtain arrangement.

Single swag with
asymmetrical cascade tails

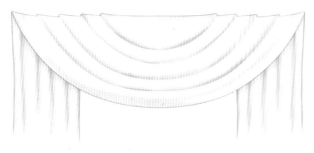

Pleated swag

Single swag with
two-tiered cascade tails

Turban swag

Single swag
with double pipe tails

Single swag with knots
and cascade tails

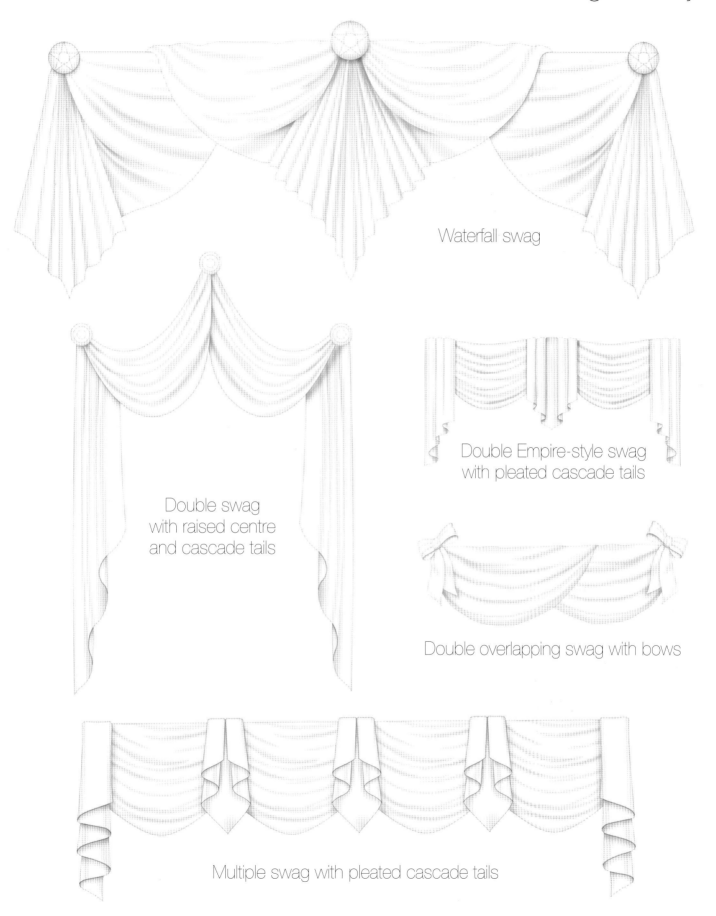

Waterfall swag

Double Empire-style swag
with pleated cascade tails

Double swag
with raised centre
and cascade tails

Double overlapping swag with bows

Multiple swag with pleated cascade tails

Hems

Essentially the finished bottom edge of a curtain or blind, hems are another area where decorative details can be added. Horizontal pleats, borders and trim help add weight and draw the eye downwards to balance an otherwise top-heavy arrangement of curtains, while scalloped edges add a pretty finish for blinds.

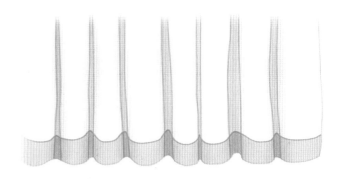

Contrasting border panel

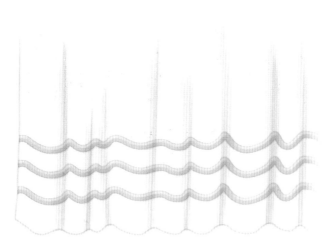

Triple rows of braids

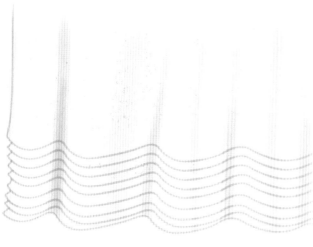

Pintucks

Rope and eyelet border

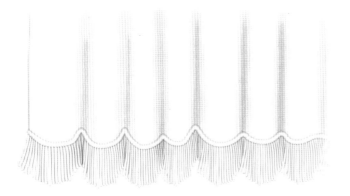

Fringing

Pleated ruffle

Gathered with rosettes

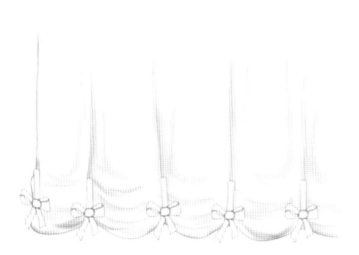

Gathered with bows

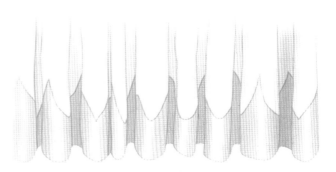

Scalloped border panel

Roller blinds

Roller blinds are made from stiffened fabric that rolls up onto a tube, which is itself attached close to the window frame on two brackets. They are simple to control, either by a spring mechanism operated by a central pull or by a side-winder chain mechanism. Roller blinds are functional and economical, can be sheer through to blackout, and can either be used alone or paired with curtains.

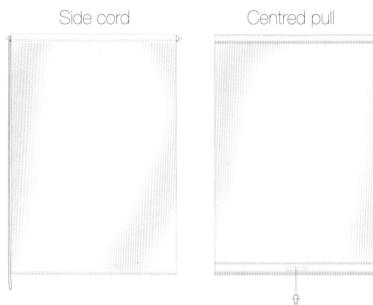

Side cord

Centred pull

With eyelets

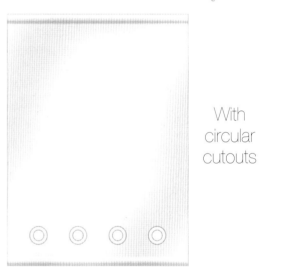

With circular cutouts

Bottom bar and scalloped tabs

Bottom bar and loop tabs

Shaped hem

Scalloped hem

Crenellated hem

Fringed
hem and
tasselled pull

Bottom bar and
semicircular cutaway

Contrasting hem with
cutout handle

Diagonal cutouts

Roman blinds

Roman blinds are flat when down, and pull up into a series of deep horizontal pleats. They are softer and less minimalist than roller blinds and can be made out of most fabrics, from unlined sheer fabrics through to heavier, blackout-lined fabrics. Roman blinds have rods attached across the back to keep them flat and are operated by a simple system of cords, which pulls the blind up from behind. More recently, this system has been replaced by a side-winder chain mechanism.

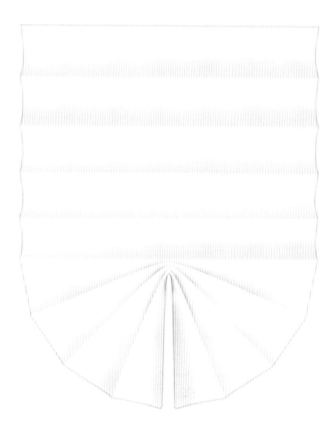

Fantail Roman blind

Pleated Roman blind

Pleated Roman blind
with contrasting border

Stiffened blind
with pin tucks

Soft Roman blind
with side ties and tassel trim

Roman blind with horizontal
stiffeners sewn into the fabric

Soft Roman blind
with pin tucks

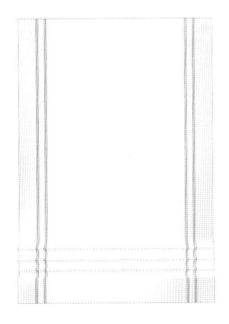

Soft Roman blind in
sheer fabric with braid

Festoon blinds

Festoon blinds are gathered or pleated across
the top of the blind to add volume to the fabric,
resulting in a softer, fuller look than either roller or
Roman blinds. Often extravagantly voluminous, they
can be made from lightweight through to heavier
fabrics and are usually cut longer than the window
so that they form pretty scoops of fabric, even
when they are fully lowered.

Twisted
single-gather blind

Single-gather blind

Fan blind

Side-gathered blind

Cascade blind

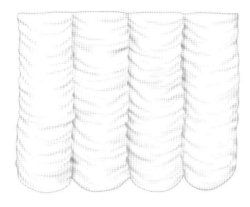

Austrian blind

Ruffled blind
with partial
Austrian gathers

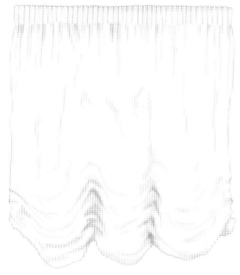

Cloud blind

Balloon

Tiered cloud blind

Balloon-tailed
blind

Roll-up and panel blinds

Roll-up blinds are very easy to operate, either with a simple cording system or by rolling up the blind by hand and tying it into place with ribbons. The handrolled versions are usually only practical when used on windows that are easy to reach. However, if access is difficult and the blinds are going to be pulled down most of the time, lightweight fabrics that allow light through are preferable. Sheer or lightweight fabrics can also be used to make panels. These are typically made with a pocket at the top and bottom so that they can be slotted onto narrow rods attached close to the window frame. Portiere panels are attached to rods that are hinged to one side of the window frame so that they operate like shutters. These can be very useful for dormer windows.

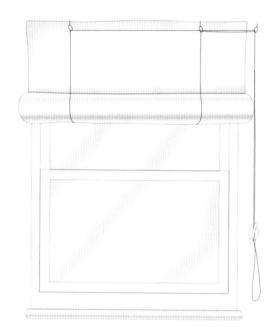

Roll-up blind

Stagecoach blind

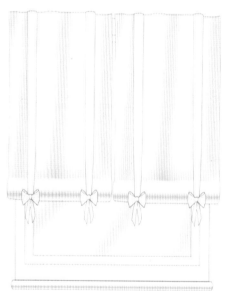

Double
stagecoach blind

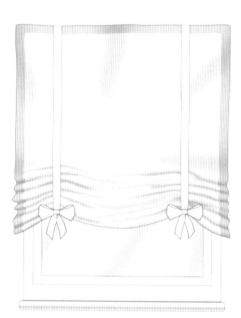

Half stagecoach blind

Sliding panels

Portiere
panel

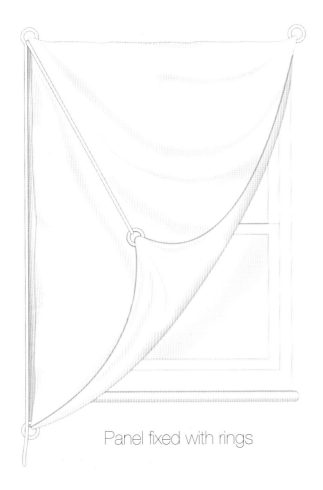

Panel fixed with rings

Ruched panel
fixed at the sides

Fixed lace panel

Shutters

Shutters are made of wood and are usually hinged to open like doors, folding back out of the way when they are not in use. Many have louvres that can be adjusted to let in varying amounts of light when the shutters are closed. Originally used in warm and sunny climates where keeping the sunlight out helped lower temperatures inside, they are usually used in place of curtains.

Simple shutters with fixed slats

Arched window with central plantation shutter and a fixed blind above

Natural-wood café shutters

Folding panel shutters

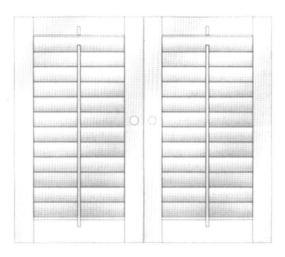

Plantation shutters,
with adjustable slats

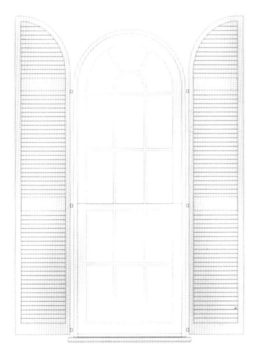

Arched plantation shutters

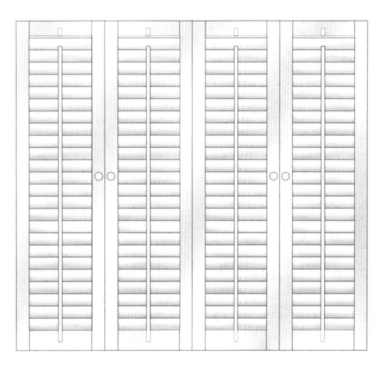

Folding plantation shutters

Rosettes, bows and fabric tiebacks

Accessories such as rosettes and bows are purely decorative, often used to adorn swags and other curtain-top treatments by adding a visual flourish. Tiebacks are more functional, holding full curtains off the windows to allow plenty of light into a room and creating a pleasing swagged shape with the curtains. In addition, tiebacks provide an opportunity for embellishment with trim, contrast borders and piping.

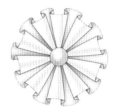

Rosette

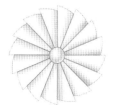

Knife-pleated rosette

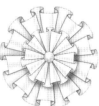

Tiered rosette

Ruffle rosette

Bow

Choux (cauliflower)

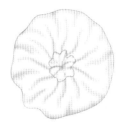

Flower rosette

Trefoil

Maltese cross

Double bow

Bow with tails

Plain fabric
tieback

Braided-edge
tieback

Rounded-end
tieback

Scalloped-edge
tieback

Puffed tieback

Fringed tieback

Plaited tieback

Shirred tieback

Smocked tieback

V-shaped tieback

Bow tieback

Ruffled tieback

Cartridge-pleated
tieback

Plain tieback with
single box pleat

With multiple
pleats

Tieback with
knife-pleated rosette

Glossary

Appliqué The technique of applying a decorative second layer of fabric onto a base cloth; decorative stitching is often used to attach the second layer.

Architrave The moulding around a window or a doorway.

Batik Fabric made using a resist-dyeing technique, originating in Indonesia where melted wax is painted onto cotton before dying.

Batten The thin piece of wood to which a blind is attached at the top, or that is slotted in at the bottom of a blind to hold the fabric straight.

'Blackout' lining A lining fabric that has been laminated to block out light. The laminate makes the lining heavier and stiffer than standard curtain lining.

Blind A window treatment that is either composed of slats or panels and made of wood, metal or vinyl, or made of flat or ruched fabric.

Bracket A support or fixture to hold up a curtain rod, track or blind. This can be decorative in the case of a wood or metal curtain rod bracket.

Bullion fringing A heavy, thick twisted fringe trimming.

Café curtain A curtain – often one that has a looped, tab or grommet heading – that covers only the bottom portion of a window.

Cascade tail An asymmetrical tail for a swag that falls into stacked pleats.

Chenille Yarn or fabric with a thick, soft, velvety pile.

Chintz A glazed cotton fabric traditionally printed with floral designs.

Contrasting border Strips of fabric of contrasting colours in various widths that are sewn onto the edges of curtains, valances and blinds.

Curtain clips Powerful clips attached to rings, usually decorative, that are used to hang a curtain from a rod.

Curtain hooks Hooks that are inserted into the back of a curtain heading as a means of support.

Cut velvet A Jacquard woven fabric with a raised velvet design on a plain background.

Damask A woven reversible fabric where the pattern is formed within the structure of the weave.

Drape The way that a fabric or curtain hangs.

Drapery arms Also known as swing arms or dormer rods, these are curtain rods that are attached to a hinged bracket at one end. Useful for dormer windows.

Draw rods A rod that clips onto the ring on the leading edge of a curtain and hangs vertically behind the curtain. Used for drawing the curtains by hand without touching the fabric.

Dress curtains Non-functional curtains that do not draw back.

Dupioni Silk or synthetic fabric with irregular thicknesses in the yarn to create a slubbed texture.

Eyelet A metal ring that lines a hole in fabric so that a rod can pass through. Eyelets are used for eyelet headings and also as a decorative feature on blinds.

Finial A decorative knob at the end of a wooden or metal curtain rod, that stops the rings from falling off the end.

Flat heading A heading, sometimes stiffened with buckram, that has no pleats or gathers.

Fringe, fringing Decorative edging with hanging threads, cords or tassels.

Gathered heading An informal curtain heading that is gathered with pull-up gathering tape.

Ground The background colour or base fabric of a printed or embroidered fabric.

Handle The texture of a fabric and the way that it drapes.

Heading tape A sew-on pull-up tape that forms various styles of curtain headings such as pencil pleats.

Holdback A decorative metal or wooden shape attached to the wall on each side of a pair of curtains that is used to hold the curtains off the window to let in more light.

Interlining A soft, thick layer inserted between the face fabric and the lining to improve the draping and insulating qualities of curtains, valances, swags and blinds.

Italian-stringing A way of drawing curtains where the heading remains stationary and the fabric is pulled back and up by means of diagonally strung cords attached behind the curtains.

Jacquard Cloth that has been woven on a Jacquard loom, where the usually elaborate pattern is formed by the structure of the weave.

Knife-edge pleat A pleated fabric or trim with small regular pleats that are pressed into sharp folds.

Lawn A fine plain-woven cotton fabric.

Leading edge The vertical edge of a curtain that will be in the middle when it is drawn.

Net pleat tape A sew- or iron-on heading tape that is transparent and used for sheer fabrics.

Organza A thin, plain-weave fabric made of silk, polyester or nylon.

Overlap Where a pair of curtains crosses over in the middle to block out light.

Pin hook Small metal hooks with one sharp end, which are pushed into the back of a hand-sewn heading.

Pinch pleat A hand-made heading pleat with two or three folds held together at the base. Pleats with three folds are called French or triple pleats.

Pipe tail A tail, that is folded into a tube rather than pleated.

Portiere A curtain that is hung in a doorway, sometimes replacing a door.

Portiere rod A metal curtain rod that is attached at one end to a door frame with a hinged bracket and at the other end to the door. When the door is opened, both the rod and the curtain rise and open too.

Recess, or window recess The area inside the frame of a window where blinds and sheer curtains can be hung.

Rep A fabric with prominent rounded crosswise ribs.

Return The gap between the front of a curtain treatment and the wall behind it. The return can be filled by the curtains or a top treatment for a neat finish and good light control.

Rod-pocket, or slotted heading A heading in which the fabric is folded over and sewn to form an open-ended channel into which a rod is inserted.

Sateen A cotton fabric made in a satin weave to give a smooth, lustrous finish that resembles satin.

Satin A smooth, lustruous fabric that is made from silk or rayon with a glossy face and dull back.

Serpentined valance A valance with a shaped lower edge that curves up and down.

Shoji screen Traditional Japanese sliding doors or screens of translucent, originally paper, panels in a wooden frame.

Slat Also known as louvre or vane – slats are the horizontal wooden, metal or vinyl parts of a blind or shutter that can be tilted to let in light.

Stackback The wall area beside a window that is covered by the curtain. The curtain 'stacks back' into this area when it is opened.

Tail A vertical tail that hangs down on each side of a swag top treatment.

Taffeta A crisp, lustrous silk or synthetic plain woven fabric.

Tension rod A rod with a spring inside that is used to hold lightweight curtains within a window recess.

Ticking A hard-wearing, striped fabric with a tightly woven herringbone weave, originally used as mattress coverings.

Tieback Crescent-shaped and stiffened fabric bands or lengths of ropes, sometimes with tassels, that are used to hold curtains back from the window.

Toile de Jouy A traditional French printed cloth, usually in one colour on a cream background depicting figurative and pastoral scenes.

Track, corded track A metal or plastic rail from which curtains are hung, sometimes corded to open and close the curtains.

Transom An architectural window term for a glass pane above a door, or the divisions within a window.

Trimming, or trim A decorative braid, fringe or tassel that is used to embellish window treatments.

Twill A type of weave, producing a hard-wearing fabric with diagonal ribs. Denim is a twill-weave fabric.

Union A fabric made from a blend of fibres – typically cotton and linen.

Velvet A rich fabric with a soft, thick pile that is made of cotton, silk or nylon.

Venetian blind A wooden or metal blind made with horizontal slats that can be lifted and lowered as well as tilted or angled to adjust light control.

Vertical blind A vinyl blind made with vertical slats that can be drawn open sideways as well as angled to adjust light control.

Practical checklist

1. Choosing fabric

When looking at fabrics for window treatments, it is not just a matter of picking something that you like the look of. Aside from design, there are other practical considerations that need to be taken into account.

- Check the fabric's cleaning instructions before purchase. Machine washing is not always an option for curtains and blinds, especially if they are too large to fit into a domestic washing machine. It can also be an issue if they are interlined, as this will shrink even if the face fabric is washable. However, if it is important to you, consider detachable linings and make sure that your chosen fabric is washable and colour-fast. Otherwise, most curtains need to be professionally dry-cleaned.
- Check the fibre content of your chosen fabric before purchase. Linens and 100 per cent cottons are prone to shrinkage, so check if they have been preshrunk and, if they haven't, allow for extra fabric in the hems.
- Check whether fabrics are fade resistant. For instance, 100 per cent silk does not perform well over time in direct sunlight and should always be used with light-protective linings and interlinings.
- Always look at fabric, especially patterned fabric, in as big a piece as possible to assess the impact of the pattern.
- Look at the fabric in natural light to gauge the true colour values, but also look at it in artificial light since colours and textures can alter significantly under different lighting.
- Gather and pleat the fabric in your hands to get an idea of how it will hang and how different types of headings will affect the pattern and texture.

2. Measuring for curtains

Whether you are making your curtains yourself or getting them made professionally, you will need to calculate the fabric quantities and estimate the costs before deciding which window treatment you want to go with. To make the calculations, you will need to have three measurements: the finished width, the finished length, and the working length. The finished width and the finished length are the lengths and widths that you want

your curtain to be when it is finished. The working length is the length that includes allowances for hems, side turnings, pleats and gathers. The following guidelines will help you take these measurements accurately.

Calculating the finished length

Decide where your curtain track or rod will be attached. This may be level with the top of the window frame or anywhere in between the top of the window frame and the ceiling, depending on the style and proportions of your room and the treatment that you are planning. For completely accurate final measurements – especially if you want your curtains to end just above the floor – it is always best to install your support first.

The finished length measurement starts at the top of a curtain track, or the bottom of the ring (or other means of hanging the curtains) on a curtain rod, and finishes where you want the bottom of the curtains to fall. For windowsill-length curtains that are to rest on the windowsill, measure to the windowsill ①. If the

---

Measuring tips

- Don't assume that any windows are exactly the same size, even if they look like they are. Measure each one individually.
- Always use an extendable steel tape measure for accurate measurements.
- Take all measurements at least twice.
- For blinds that hang inside a window frame or recess, don't assume that windows are perfectly rectangular. Measure the width in several places and use the narrowest measurement as the final width.
- Don't assume that floors and ceilings are level. Take your length measurement in several places across the width, and if there is a slight variation, use the shortest measurement. If there is a big discrepancy, it may be necessary to hang your curtains unhemmed and to pin up the hems in situ.

curtains are to hang just below the windowsill, add 10–15 cm (4–6 in), depending on the proportions of the window and whether there is a radiator, for instance. For floor-length curtains ②, measure to the floor and, if they are to hang just above floor level, take 1 cm ($^1/_3$ in) off. For curtains that are intended to break on the floor, add 1.5 cm (½ in) to the floor measurement. For curtains that are intended to pool on the floor, add about 10–25 cm (4–10 in).

Calculating the finished width

Measure the window widthways and then add a 5-cm (2-in) allowance for overlaps where a pair of curtains meets in the middle ③. You may occasionally need to add an allowance for returns ④, ⑤, if you want your curtains to return back to the wall from the track or rod. This is especially important in a bedroom where light control is required. In this example, allow 10 cm (4 in) for returns on each side, or whatever the distance is between the track or rod and the wall behind it.

To calculate drops

A drop is a width of fabric – some wide curtains might be made up of as many as six or seven widths of fabric sewn together. If you're hanging a single narrow curtain that is made up of just one drop, omit this part of the calculation.

- To work out the number of drops, multiply the finished width measurement by the amount of fullness that you require. In part, this depends on the kind of heading you have chosen (see below). This is not an exact science, and it will also depend on your fabric choice and the look you are trying to create. As a guideline, multiplying your width by two will give you adequately full curtains.

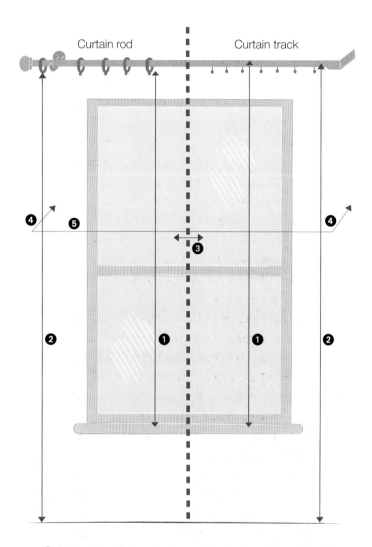

Curtain rod   Curtain track

① finished length from bottom of ring (or top of track) to sill
② finished length from bottom of ring (or top of track) to floor
③ overlap
④ return
⑤ finished width including returns and overlap

curtain heading type	drop measurement
gathered headings, rod-pocket headings, eyelet headings, tab headings	1½ to 2 times the width
cartridge pleats	2 times the width
pinch pleats, goblet pleats	2 to 2½ times the width
pencil pleats, box pleats	2½ to 3 times the width

- Multiply the finished width by the relevant number for your heading. Divide the resulting number by the width of your fabric – usually 137 cm (54 in) – to ascertain the number of drops you will need for each curtain. You will have to round this figure up or down to the nearest half-width of fabric.

To calculate the working length

- Add an allowance for hems and headings to your finished length measurement. This is usually 30–40 cm (12–16 in). This will give you the working length. Multiply the working length number by the number of drops required. If you are using plain fabric that has no repeated pattern, this final figure indicates the amount of fabric you require. If you are using a patterned fabric, read the point below to find out how to allow for a repeated pattern.

Example: For pinch-pleated curtains with a finished width of 150 cm (59 in) and a drop of 240 cm (94 in):

Multiply the finished width by the amount of fullness to get the full width: 150 cm x 2½ = 375 cm (59 in x 2½ = 147 in). Divide the full width by the width of the fabric: 375 cm / 137 cm (147 in / 54 in) = 2.7. Round this up to three drops. Add the drop to the hem and heading allowance to give you the working length: 240 cm + 40 cm = 280 cm (94 in + 16 in = 110 in). Multiply the working length by 3: 280 cm x 3 = 840 cm (110 in x 3 = 330 in). So you will need 8.4 m (9.1 yards) of fabric to complete the job.

3. To calculate the pattern repeat allowance

- The pattern repeat is the vertical distance between any given point in a design and where that exact point is repeated again. When you are using more than one drop of fabric, you need to connect the fabric so that the pattern matches across the full width of the curtains and matches up at the seams. You have to allow for extra fabric in order to do this. Knowing the distance between the pattern repeats on the fabric is vital in order to be able to connect patterned fabric and is also key in determining how much extra fabric to buy. Ask your supplier for the pattern repeat measurement – or measure this yourself between two points on the pattern where the pattern starts to repeat itself. To work out how much extra fabric is needed for a pair of curtains, divide the working length measurement by the pattern repeat and round up the resulting number to the next whole number. Multiply this figure by the pattern repeat. The result will be your working length measurement including the pattern repeat

allowance. Proceed as you would for unpatterned fabrics by multiplying your working length measurement by the required number of drops.

Example: For curtains that are 150 cm (59 in) wide and 240 cm (94 in) long with a pattern repeat of 65 cm (25½ in):

Divide the working length of 280 cm (110 in) by the pattern repeat: 280 cm / 65 cm (110 in / 25½ in) = 4.3. Round this up to 5 and multiply by the pattern repeat to get the working length including pattern repeat: 5 x 65 cm = 325 cm (25½ in x 5 = 127½ in). Multiply this by 3 (no of drops required). 325 cm x 3 = 975 cm (127½ in x 3 = 382½ in). So you will need a total of 9.75 m (10.6 yd) of fabric.

4. Measuring for blinds

Working out the finished length

- First decide exactly where the blind is to be hung. Decide if you would like to cover the entire window and frame or if you want to leave some of the frame uncovered. If a window opens inwards, make sure that the blind is hung sufficiently high to allow the window to open without obstruction. If the window is deeply recessed it is common to position the blind as close to the glass as possible within the recess.

- Next, decide exactly where the blind will end – if it is to land on the windowsill when it is down, then it should end at the windowsill; if you want it to hang in front of the sill, then it should end just below it.

- Once you have decided on the position of the top of the blind, measure from that point to the windowsill or just below it. This will give you a finished length measurement. For wooden or aluminium Venetian blinds or for vertical blinds, this is the only length measurement that you will need.

To calculate the working length

- For fabric blinds, add 15–20 cm (6–8 in) to the finished length measurement for hems and then add extra, depending on the style of the blind. Roller blinds need an extra 15–20 cm (6–8 in) to ensure that there is always fabric rolled around the roller, even when the blind is fully down. Blinds such as Austrian blinds need up to 30 cm (12 in) extra so that the fullness remains in the blind even when it is fully down. Once you have added these allowances, you will have your working length measurement.

Working out the finished width

- To obtain the finished width measurement, measure from one side to the other the area you intend the blind to cover.
- The brackets of roller blinds sit on either side of the roller, so it is vital that you know how much allowance to leave for the brackets, especially if the blind is to be hung in a recess. Venetian and vertical blinds hang from a box or track, and your manufacturer will give you details on how much clearance is required for hanging these.
- For fabric blinds that will have a hem on either side, add 10 cm (4 in) to the finished width measurement to allow for the hems.
- Austrian and cloud blinds have fullness across the width that is formed either by curtain tape attached to the back or by the addition of inverted pleats. Calculate the working width measurement by multiplying the finished width by the required amount of fullness (see heading calculations above) for taped headings. For pleats, decide how many pleats and how deep they will be, double the pleat width measurement, multiply it by the number of pleats, and add the result to the finished width measurements.
- In some cases, blinds will require more than one width of fabric. To find out how many widths are needed, divide the width of the fabric (usually 137 cm or 54 in) by the working width of the blind. Round up the result to the next whole number and that will give you the number of drops you will need.
- Multiply the working length measurement by the number of drops to calculate the total amount of fabric you will need. If your fabric has a pattern, refer to the section above on pattern repeats to calculate the additional fabric you will need.

5. Do-it-yourself or professional?

Here are some points to consider when it comes to doing the work:

Do-it-yourself

Many simple styles are within the capabilities of an amateur – and there is great satisfaction to be gained from making your window treatments yourself. If you are using elaborate treatments and expensive fabrics, however, it may be best to leave it to the professionals. For blinds, you can buy kits that supply all the necessary hardware.

Readymade

Today many straightforward curtains and blinds are available readymade. They only come in standard sizes, but they are much less expensive than custom-made equivalents. In the case of blinds, some can easily be cut down to fit.

Custom-made

Interior designers and custom workrooms will take on the job from start to finish. This is the most expensive option, but it is often necessary for elaborate treatments and difficult windows. This option should give excellent professional results.

Hiring professionals

Whether you are hiring an interior designer or a professional curtain maker, some points are worth considering in advance:

- Personal recommendations are often the best route, so ask friends who have had similar work done. Alternatively, ask your fabric retailer for recommendations or search the Internet for trade associations with members in your area.
- Ask to see portfolios and references.
- Be specific about what you want – take time beforehand to think about the project carefully and be as clear as possible. The clearer your brief, the less chance of a misunderstanding.
- Get at least two estimates and make sure that you know exactly what the estimate includes. Remember that very low estimates may not result in the best job.
- Put it in writing. Make sure that everything is on paper and record any updates if you change your mind at a later date.

Useful addresses

The following list of manufacturers, associations, and outlets is meant to be a general guide to additional industry and product-related sources. It is not intended as a complete listing of products and manufacturers represented in this book.

Associations

Association of Master Upholsterers & Soft Furnishers
Provides advice service for consumers
Francis Vaughan House
Q1 Capital Point Business
Centre, Capital Business Park
Parkway, Cardiff CF3 2PU
Tel: 0292 077 8918
www.upholsterers.co.uk

British Blind & Shutter Association
Represents UK blind and shutter manufacturers
42 Heath Street
Tamworth
Staffordshire B79 7JH
Tel: 01827 52337
wwww.bbsa.org.uk

Blinds and shutters

Amazing Shutters
Unit 10&11
1750 Steeles Avenue W
Concord, ON L4K 2L7
Canada
Tel: +1 905 660 1127
www.amazingshutter.com

Aveno Window Fashions
4795 Fulton Industrial
Boulevard, Atlanta, GA 30336
USA
Tel: +1 404 505 1501
www.aveno.com

Eclectics
Pyramid Business Park
Poorhole Lane, Broadstairs
Kent CT10 2PT
Tel: 01843 608789
www.eclectics.co.uk

Hunter Douglas Inc
2 Park Way & Route 17 South
P.O. Box 740
Upper Saddle River
New Jersey, NJ 07458
USA
Tel: +1 800 789 0331
www.hunterdouglas.com

Kirsch Window Fashions
4110 Premier Drive
High Point, NC 27265
USA
Tel: + 1 800 817 6344
www.kirsch.com

Levolor Window Fashions
4110 Premier Drive
High Point, NC 27265
USA
Tel: +1 800 538 6567
www.levolor.com

Talius
7401 Pacific Circle
Mississauga, ON L5T 2A4
Canada
Tel: +1 800 665 5553
www.talius.com

Fabric and soft treaments

Alhambra
P. Las Atalayas
c/ del Marco, 61
03114 Alicante
Spain
Tel: +34 965 107 004
www.alhambraint.com

Benartex
Suite 1100, 8th Floor
1359 Broadway
New York, NY 10018
USA
Tel: +1 212 840 3250
www.benartex.com

Blendworth
Crookley Park, Horndean
Hampshire PO8 0AD
Tel: 023 9259 4911
www.blendworth.co.uk

J.R. Burrows & Co.
P.O. Box 522, Rockland
Massachusetts, MA 02370
USA
Tel: +1 800 347 1795 /
+ 1 781 982 1812
www.burrows.com

Calico Corners
203 Gale Lane, Kennett
Square, PA 19348
USA
Tel: +1 800 213 6366
www.calicocorners.com

The Cloth Shop
290 Portobello Road
London W10 5TE
Tel: 020 8968 6001

Country Curtains
Red Lion Inn, 30 Main Street,
PO Box 954, Stockbridge
MA 01262-0954, USA
Tel: +1 800 456 0321
www.countrycurtains.com

Croscill Home Fashions
25th Floor, 261 Fifth Avenue
New York, NY 10016
USA
Tel: +1 212 689 7222
www.croscill.com

Designers Guild
277 Kings Road
London SW3 5EN
Tel: 020 7351 5775
www.designersguild.com

Globaltex
Unit 2, The Madison Centre
Knowsley Road, Haslingden
Lancashire BB4 4EG
Tel: 01706 242010
www.globaltex.co.uk

Harlequin Harris
Chelsea Harbour Design
Centre, London SW10 0XE
Tel: 08708 300032
www.harlequinharris.com

Hornsby Interiors
35 Thurloe Place
London SW7 2HJ
Tel: 020 7255 2888
sales@hornsbyinteriors.com

Ian Mankin
109 Regents Park Road
London NW1 8UR
Tel: 020 7722 0997
www.ianmankin.com

Jane Churchill
110 Fulham Road
London SW3 6HU
Tel: 020 7244 7427
www.janechurchill.com

Kobe
Loddon Vale House
Hurricane Way, Woodley
Berkshire RG5 4UX
Tel: 0118 969 1020
www.kobe.eu

Old World Weavers
D&D Building
979 Third Avenue
New York, NY 10022
USA
Tel: +1 212 752 9000
www.old-world-weavers.com

Prestigious Textiles
4 Cross Lane
Westgate Hill Street
Bradford BD4 0SG
Tel:01274 688448
www.prestigious.co.uk

Romanzia
655 County Road A
P.O. Box 72
Chetek, WI 54728
USA
Tel: +1 715 924 2960
www.romanzia.com

Romo Fabrics
Chelsea Harbour Design
Centre, London SW10 0XE
Tel: 01623 756699
www.romofabrics.com

Spiegel
Spiegel Customer Satisfaction
1 Spiegel Avenue
Hampton, VA 23630, USA
Tel: +1 800 474 5555
www.spiegel.com

Stroheim & Romann
30-30 47th Avenue
New York, NY 11101, USA
Tel: +1 718 706 7000
www.stroheim.com

Universal Draperies
114 Advance Boulevard
Brampton, ON L6T 4J4
Canada
Tel: +1 800 265 5127
www.universaldraperies.com

Villa Nova Fabrics
Lowmoor Road,
Kirkby-in-Ashfield
Nottinghamshire NG17 7DE
Tel: 01623 756699
www.villanova.co.uk

Warris Vianni
85 Golborne Road
London W10 5NL
Tel: 020 8964 0069
www.warrisvianni.com

Warwick Fabrics
Hackling House
Bourton Industrial Park
Bourton-on-the-water
Gloucs GL54 2HQ
Tel: 01451 822383
www.warwick.co.uk

Waverly
Tel: +1 800 423 5881
www.waverly.com

Hardware

Atlas Homewares
326 Mira Loma Avenue
Glendale, CA 91204
USA
Tel: +1 800 799 6755
www.atlashomewares.com

The Bradley Collection Ltd
Lion Barn, Maitland Road
Needham Market
Suffolk IP6 8NS
Tel: 0845 118 7224
www.bradleycollection.co.uk

Freder Textiles
550 Montpelier
Montreal, QB H4N 2G7
Canada
Tel: +1 800 361 5920
www.fredertextiles.com

Graber Window Fashions
Cathedral City, CA
USA
Tel: +1 888 684 7890
www.graber.ws

Hunter & Hyland
201–5 Kingston Road
Leatherhead,
Surrey KT22 7PB
Tel: 01372 378511
www.hunterandhyland.co.uk

Integra Products Ltd
Eastern Avenue, Lichfield
Staffordshire WS13 7SB
Tel: 01543 267100
www.integra-products.co.uk

Ona Drapery Company
5320 Arapahoe Avenue
Boulder, CO 80303, USA
Tel: +1 800 231 4025
www.onadrapery.com

Sunflex
Keys Park Road,
Hednesford, Cannock
Staffordshire WS12 2FR
Tel: 01543 271421
www.sunflex.co.uk

Trimmings

Flecotex
C/ Duquesa de Almodóvar
6–03830 Muro del Alcoy
Alicante, Spain
Tel: +34 96 654 40 32
www.flecotex.com

**Newark Dressmaker Supply
and Home-Sew**
P.O. Box 4099, Bethlehem,
PA 18018-0099, USA
Tel: +1 800 344 4739
www.homesew.com

Rashmishree
B-37, South Extension – II,
First Floor, New Delhi 110049,
India
Tel: +91 11 2625 4743 /
+ 91 11 2625 7020
www.rashmishreegroup.com

Sevinch
1403, 15 Hassan Sabry Street
Zamalek, Cairo 11211
Egypt
Tel: +20 2735 3439
www.passementerie.org

Index

Acknowledgments

The publishers would like to thank the following companies for their invaluable assistance: Alhambra, Blendworth, The Bradley Collection, Calico Corners, Country Curtains, eclectics, Globaltex, Hunter Douglas Associates Inc., Hunter & Hyland, Integra Products Ltd, Jim Lawrence Traditional Ironwork Ltd, Kobe, Lou Hammond & Associates, Prestigious Textiles, Stroheim & Romann, Sunflex, Villa Nova, Warwick Fabrics.

All material swatches were taken from the author's own collection but illustrate the fabrics of Ian Mankin, Hornsby Interiors, Harlequin Fabrics, Romo Fabrics, Jane Churchill, Warris Vianni, The Cloth Shop, John Lewis and the Designers Guild among others.

Photos

2 Villa Nova/Romo Fabrics
6–7 Kobe
8 *bottom left* Corbis/Christophe Boisivieux
9 *top* Getty Images/The Bridgeman Art Library; *bottom* Art Archive
10 *top* Andreas von Einsiedel/Architects: Guard, Tillman, Pollock Ltd; *bottom* Country Curtains
11 Roller blind in 'Ambience' solar-reflective fabric from eclectics
12 Andreas von Einsiedel/Designer: Candy & Candy
13 *left* Blendworth; *right* Villa Nova/Romo Fabrics
14 Villa Nova/Romo Fabrics
22–23 Grant Govier/Redcover.com
24 Andreas von Einsiedel/Designer: Michael Reeves; *blind swatches* Sunflex
25 Warwick Fabrics
26 Blendworth
27 Graham Atkins-Hughes/Redcover.com

28 Graham Atkins-Hughes/Redcover.com
29 Graham Atkins-Hughes/Redcover.com; *curtain rings* The Bradley Collection
30 Warwick Fabrics
31 Andreas von Einsiedel/Designer: Ernest de la Torre; *rods* Integra Products
32 Alhambra
33 Andreas von Einsiedel/Designer: Rose Uniacke
34 The Bradley Collection
35 Andreas von Einsiedel/Designer: Luz Vargas Architects
36 Warwick Fabrics
37 Silhouette® window shadings from Hunter Douglas
38 Dan Duchars/Redcover.com
39 Luminette® privacy sheers from Hunter Douglas
40–41 Alhambra
42 Silhouette® window shadings from Hunter Douglas; *tiebacks* Price & Co.
43 Calico Corners

44 Andreas von Einsiedel/Designer: Annie Constantine
45 Calico Corners
46 Martyn O'Kelly/Redcover.com
47 Henry Wilson/Redcover.com; *holdbacks* Country Curtains
48 Calico Corners; *rods* Integra Products
49 Christopher Drake/Redcover.com Architect/Designer: Philip Wagner; *finials* Integra Products
50 Calico Corners; *poles 1 & 3* Hunter & Hyland; *pole 2* Integra Products
51 Redcover.com
52 Andreas von Einsiedel/Designer: Charles Style; *holdback* Integra Products
53 Rob Marmion/Fotolia.com; *holdbacks* Büsche
54 Andreas von Einsiedel/Designer: Homeira Pour-Heidari
55 Country Woods® Exposé™ wood blinds from Hunter Douglas; *rods* Integra Products
56 Henry Wilson/Redcover.com

57 Kobe

58 Andreas von Einsiedel/Designer: Alison Henry; *tassels* Sevinch (Michael Deman)

59 Andreas von Einsiedel/Designer: John Simpson

60–61 Andreas von Einsiedel/Designer: Smiros & Smiros Architects

62 Integra Products; *rope tiebacks* Country Curtains

63 Mike Daines/Redcover.com

64 Alhambra

65 Somner® collection custom vertical blinds from Hunter Douglas

66 Andreas von Einsiedel/Designer: Sue Timney

67 Integra Products; *rods* Sunflex

68 Paul Massey/Redcover.com

69 Andreas von Einsiedel/Designer: Andrew McAlpine

70 Verity Welstead/Redcover.com

71 Guglielmo Galvin/Redcover.com

72 Villa Nova/Romo Fabrics

73 Chalet Woods® wood blinds from Hunter Douglas; *finials* Integra Products

74 Anthony Harrison/Redcover.com

75 Prestigious Textiles; *fringes 1 & 2* Price & Co; *fringe 3* Newark Dressmaker

76–77 Chris Drake/Redcover.com

78 Amanda Turner/Redcover.com

79 Country Curtains

80 Blendworth

81 Dan Duchars/Redcover.com; *tieback* Country Curtains

82 Stroheim & Romann

83 Country Curtains; *rods* Integra Products

84 Calico Corners

85 Country Curtains

86 Marcus Wilson-Smith/Redcover.com Designer: Moussie Sayer

87 Villa Nova/Romo Fabrics; *pins* Country Curtains

88 Stroheim & Romann

89 Cadence® soft vertical blinds from Hunter Douglas

90 Christopher Drake/Redcover.com Architect/Designer: Philip Wagner

91 Christopher Drake/Redcover; *clip* Country Curtains

92–93 Calico Corners

94 Country Curtains

95 Country Curtains; *scarf holder 1* Jones & Co; *scarf holders 2 & 3* Integra Products

96 Alhambra

97 Kobe; *finials* The Bradley Collection

98 Country Curtains

99 Villa Nova/Romo Fabrics; *rods* Integra Products

100 Alhambra

101 Andreas von Einsiedel/Designer: Catherine Warren; *rods* Jim Lawrence

102 Duette® honeycomb shades from Hunter Douglas

103 Andreas von Einsiedel/Designer: Kenyon Kramer; *rods* Hunter & Hyland

104 Silhouette® window shadings from Hunter Douglas

105 Luminette® privacy sheers from Hunter Douglas; *blind swatches* Sunflex

106 Andreas von Einsiedel/Designer Tom Newby

107 Andreas von Einsiedel/Designer: Robert Boswell; *tassels* Flecotex

108 Jim Lawrence

109 Jim Lawrence

110 Globaltex

111 Simon McBride/Redcover.com

112–113 The EverWood® collection of alternative wood blinds from Hunter Douglas

114 Prestigious Textiles; *finials* The Bradley Collection

115 Provenance® woven wooden shades from Hunter Douglas

116 Stroheim & Romann; *rods* Büsche

117 Silhouette® window shadings from Hunter Douglas

118 Blendworth

119 Graham Atkins-Hughes/Redcover.com

120 Remembrance® window shades from Hunter Douglas

121 Villa Nova/Romo Fabrics

122 Prestigious Textiles

123 Prestigious Textiles

124 Blendworth

125 Alhambra; *finials* The Bradley Collection

126–127 Marcus Wilson-Smith/Redcover.com

128 Andreas von Einsiedel/Designer: Lia Martinucci; *rods* Hunter & Hyland

129 Country Woods® Exposé™ wood blinds from Hunter Douglas

130 Andreas von Einsiedel/Designer: Sallie Jeeves; *rods* Hunter & Hyland

131 Kobe

132 Warwick Fabrics

133 Andreas von Einsiedel/Designer: Carolinda Tolstoy

134 Andreas von Einsiedel/Designer: Hudson Featherstone Architects; *draw rods* The Bradley Collection

135 Vignette® modern Roman shades from Hunter Douglas

136 Mark Bolton/Redcover.com; *rods* Jim Lawrence

137 Country Woods® Exposé™ wood blinds from Hunter Douglas

138 Duette® honeycomb shades from Hunter Douglas

139 Mel Yates/Redcover.com; *hooks & clips* Hunter & Hyland

140–141 Vignette® modern Roman shades from Hunter Douglas

142 Alhambra

143 Winfried Heinze/Redcover.com; *curved rod* The Bradley Collection

144 Silhouette® window shadings from Hunter Douglas

145 Dan Duchars/Redcover.com

146 Verity Welstead/Redcover.com

147 Calico Corners

148 Applause® honeycomb shades from Hunter Douglas

149 Robin Matthews/Redcover.com; *tiebacks* Sunflex

150 Alun Callender/Redcover.com

151 Johnny Bouchier/Redcover.com

152 Applause® honeycomb shades from Hunter Douglas

153 Johnny Bouchier/Redcover.com; *finial* Hunter & Hyland

154–179 Illustrations by Mark Franklin based on originals by Elsa Godfry

Other illustrations by Ana Maria